Essential Ásatrú

Other Books by Diana L. Paxson

Essential Ásatrú

A Modern Guide to Norse Paganism

DIANA L. PAXSON

CITADEL PRESS
Kensington Publishing Corp.
www.kensingtonbooks.com

CITADEL PRESS BOOKS are published by

Kensington Publishing Corp.
119 West 40th Street
New York, NY 10018

Copyright © 2006, 2021 Diana L. Paxson

All Kensington titles, imprints, and distributed lines are available at special quantity discounts for bulk purchases for sales promotions, premiums, fund-raising, educational, or institutional use. Special book excerpts or customized printings can also be created to fit specific needs. For details, write or phone the office of the Kensington sales manager: Kensington Publishing Corp., 119 40th Street, New York, NY 10018, attn: Sales Department; phone 1-800-221-2647.

CITADEL PRESS and the Citadel logo are Reg. U.S. Pat. & TM Off.

First printing: December 2006
Fourteenth printing (updated edition): March 2021

22 21 20 19 18 17 16 15

Printed in the United States of America

ISBN-13: 978-0-8065-4112-9
ISBN-10: 0-8065-4112-1

Electronic edition:

ISBN-13: 978-0-8065-4113-6 (e-book)
ISBN-10: 0-8065-4113-X (e-book)

Contents

Foreword

When *Essential Ásatrú* was published in 2006, the idea that paganism is a viable modern faith was still new to the general public and the only tradition that most people had heard of was Wicca. However many pagans were already seeking a religious practice more firmly rooted in authentic cultural traditions, including Greek, Roman, Celtic and Germanic. The first, and I believe still the biggest of these "Reconstructionist" religions to gain popular recognition is Ásatrú, or to use a broader term, "Heathenry," the pre-Christian religion of the Germanic-speaking peoples. The faith continues to flourish today. In Iceland an Ásatrú temple is nearing completion. In Europe and the Americas, heathen groups have increased their numbers, resources and understanding of our religion.

I have now been active in the heathen community for twice as long as I had been when this book was written, serving as a leader in the Troth and my kindred. The general character of Heathenry as portrayed here remains the same. What has changed for this tradition, as it has for so many other aspects of Euro-American culture, is the relationship between identity and ancestry. Today, there is an ever-widening divide between Folkish Heathens who believe that Ásatrú should be practiced only by people of Northern European descent, and Inclusive Heathens who believe that what matters is not ancestry but affinity.

People come to Heathenry for many reasons. Some are looking for a faith they can practice without fear of misappropriation. Others want to reclaim traditions lost when families of Germanic descent rejected their heritage during the World Wars. Some encounter Thor in a movie and think he's cool. Still others are drawn by the old Germanic values and worldview. There are those who are attracted by heathen community spirit, and there are those who come because they have had a Close Encounter with one of the gods.

Contemporary Heathenry is a constructed culture. Our first goal may be to improve our connection to Spirit, but people also need a community with which they can share companionship and values. Whatever their ancestry, all heathens must learn a new culture. Inclusive kindreds welcome newcomers of whatever origin in the same way that the United States naturalizes new citizens, through education about our history and acculturation to our ways.

Heathenry, like other "Earth Religions," is based on traditional values and the triad of the gods, the ancestors, and the land. Gods and myths are specific to each pagan tradition, but most revere their Ancestors. Inclusive Heathens honor our ancestors of the flesh or of the spirit not because they are Northern European, but because they are ours. We honor the spirits of the land on which we live, and recognize our responsibility to care for it.

In this book you will find information on Heathenry past and present and an updated list of resources for further and deeper exploration. In the vignettes of the (mythical) Ravenhammer Kindred, you will meet the kinds of people you may encounter in the heathen community.

Hail and welcome!

Introduction

In 2000, I was invited to give a paper on Scandinavian oracular practice at the Viking Symposium in Newfoundland. Most of the presenters were from various universities. My name tag stated that I was from "the Troth." "What's that?" asked a lady as we were waiting for dinner. "A heathen religious organization," I replied. She gave me a confused look—"Isn't that a contradiction in terms?" At that point, I realized I was going to have to preface my paper by defining what I meant both by *heathen* and *religion*. Since then, I've participated in numerous discussions in which modern pagans of all flavors struggled to define themselves, so it seems wise to begin this book by defining some basic terms.

Pagan Religions

Just as Christianity, Judaism, and Islam can be grouped together as monotheistic "Abrahamic" religions that believe in a single all-powerful god, polytheistic religions that honor a multitude of deities also form religious "families." Among them we find the myriad Hindu sects, Buddhism, which is nontheistic in its theology but includes polytheistic elements in its practice, tribal traditions from the Americas and Asia, the African and Afro-diasporic faiths, which include modern Umbanda and Santeria, and European paganism.

Until very recently, the possibility that a Native European

polytheistic faith could be a viable option would have been met with incomprehension. Today, however, a linear worldview that includes an inevitable progress (?) toward a cataclysm decreed by a single, all-powerful God is proving dangerously attractive to some, and to the rest of us, simply dangerous. Instead of a worldview in which neither humanity nor nature have intrinsic meaning because all such meaning derives only from God, or polarizes into a conflict between absolute Good and absolute Evil, we need a worldview that sees holiness in everything, recognizes that spirit takes many forms, and believes that history moves in circles, not a straight line (for an excellent examination of this question, see John Michael Greer's *A World Full of Gods*, 2005).

The first European polytheistic religion to become well known in Europe and North America in the twentieth century was Pagan Witchcraft, or Wicca, which includes a multitude of traditions derived from or inspired by survivals from European folk religion and the work of Gerald Gardner (see Bonewits, 2001). However, Wicca is by no means the only kind of European paganism to flourish today. A second, and rapidly growing, branch of the family consists of the "reconstructed" traditions based on the practices and beliefs of specific cultures. These include the Celtic traditions, among them the different kinds of Druids; the Hellenic traditions, which draw from ancient Greece; the Kemetics, who base their practice on the religion of Egypt; Baltic traditionalists, who have revived their native religions in their newly independent nations; and the religions of the Germanic peoples in Scandinavia, on the Continent, and in England.

Heathen Faith

Just as traditional cultures tend to call themselves "the People," their religions are generally known as something like "our way," if they are called anything at all. Thus, it was not until Christians began their attempt to convert the North that the Germanic peoples needed a name for their beliefs. Churchmen called the religion, and its followers, heathen. When scholars and romantics began to study the old ways in the nineteenth century, some called it the "troth," or faith, of the gods—*Ásatrú*. Either term, or a number of others, from the "Northern Way," to "Norse paganism," "Irminism," "Forn Sidhr" or "Forn Sed" (Old Custom), "Theodism," "Germanic Reconstructionism," the "Elder Troth," or "Odinism/Wotanism" (although the latter may give the erroneous impression that Odin is the only god), can be used for the versions of Germanic religion that we are attempting to recover and re-create today.

Until recently, the term *heathen*, like *pagan*, was taken to mean a person without religion, or at least without the civilizing influence of Christianity. The word was first recorded in the translation of the Bible into Gothic made by Ulfilas in the fourth century, where it was used to translate the term *Gentile*. It has been assumed that just as *pagan* meant the people of the "pagus" or countryside, *heathen* meant the people of the heath who continued to practice the old ways when the city folk had all converted to Christianity. This interpretation has been questioned; however, *heathen* is at least a term that modern English speakers can both recognize and spell, and one that, moreover, can be found in all the Germanic languages. On the other hand, it can also be used, or misunderstood, as a pejorative.

As a name, the term *Ásatrú* has the advantage of being both distinctive and easily recognized. It is a word from Old Norse, the language in which most of the surviving Germanic religious lore was written. It also has the distinction of being the name by which the only state-supported (as opposed to legal) pagan religious organization is known. Appropriately enough, Iceland, the last country in which the Aesir (the Norse gods and goddesses) were officially worshipped, was also the first to restore official recognition of Ásatrú as a modern religion. The Ásatrúarfelagidh, or Ásatrú Fellowship, was established after the faith was recognized in 1972. As of 2018, over 4,000 Icelanders had registered with the Felagidh, which receives a portion of the church tax each year. In a country with a population of around

200,000, this number is significant, and I am told that it is steadily increasing.

Of course, the term *Ásatrú* also presents some difficulties. Just as the word *man* (which in the old Germanic languages was a neutral, not a masculine, term) is today used for all humans as well as for males, the word *æsir* can include all the deities, just the males, or only those from the clan who live in Asgard. There are also some who use *Ásatrú* to designate those who worship the Norse gods only, avoiding involvement with any other tradition. For example, Theodists who follow the Anglo-Saxon or Continental Germanic tribal traditions generally consider themselves heathen but not Ásatrú. When I use the term by itself in this book, it will refer to the worship of all the northern deities. I will also be using the words "Ásatrú" and "Heathen" more or less interchangeably.

Heathen, like the word *Lutheran*, can be used as a noun or an adjective, as in "I am a heathen," "A Heathen ritual." The collective term for the religion would be "Heathenism," and for Heathens as a group, "Heathenry." Capitalization seems to be optional. "Asatrù" can also be either a noun or an adjective, but the same term, capitalized in the singular, is used for the religion or the collective. For more than one adherent, however, we use the Norse plural, "Ásatrúar."

Like witches, heathens have to contend with negative stereotypes and associations from the past. The first display case in the Smithsonian Institution's Viking Exhibition featured some of them, from operatic horned helmets to a helmet from the Minnesota Vikings. True, there are heathen bikers, but not all heathens ride motorcycles or even drink beer. Some prison gang members may call themselves Asatrù, but in ordinary life, Ásatrúar are likely to be among the most law-abiding and responsible members of a community. Although some liberal watchdogs have tried to define the Thor's hammer as a hate symbol, most of those who wear it are as positive in their outlook as those witches who wear the pentagram.

Looking for the Lore

What did the heathens of old believe, and how did they practice their religion? No recovered pagan tradition has complete information on the practices of the past, but Ásatrú is fortunate in possessing a large body of material, known as "the lore", on which to draw for inspiration.

Our major sources for the reconstruction of heathen religion are the poetic and prose *Edda*—poems and stories based on the myths that were written down in thirteenth-century Iceland, though the stories themselves are far older; epics such as *Beowulf* and other early Continental literature; the *sagas*—multigenerational "novels" about the early Icelanders that include fascinating references to heathen magic and religious practice; the histories written by early medieval authors such as Snorri Sturlusson, Saxo Grammaticus, Jordanes, and others about their countries' recent and not-so-recent heathen pasts; and collections of folklore by Jacob Grimm and others. In addition, there have been a variety of modern historical and literary studies, to which I will be referring.

Some call Ásatrú "the religion with homework." If you are interested in learning more, I recommend the resources listed at the end of this book, in particular *Our Troth*, which covers much of the material included here in far greater detail, and provides full references to the scholarly sources.

Who This Book Is For

This book is an introduction to heathen faith and practice. It is intended for the reader who is simply curious about Germanic religion, who may be acquainted with Wicca and would like to know what else is out there, or who has a friend or relative who has gotten involved with Ásatrú and wants to know why. If you are already a practicing heathen, you will probably find the content familiar, though some of the perspectives may be new. In a book of this size, only the most essential information could be included. I have tried to compensate by listing a variety of more comprehensive sources in the section on resources. Whether you are new to Heathenry or an old hand, I encourage you to explore them.

Acknowledgments

We do not walk the path of Ásatrú alone. To be heathen is to walk with the gods and goddesses and my brothers and sisters in the faith as we create and re-create our community. Certainly, I could never have written this book without the insights, opinions, commentary, and occasional opposition of the many heathens I have worked with in my own kindred and the larger heathen community over the years.

In particular, I would like to honor Paul Edwin Zimmer, Laurel Mendes, Kveldulf Gundarsson, Bill Bainbridge, Rob Schreiwer, and Lorrie Wood for their inspiration and support, and to thank Ben Waggoner for his many valuable suggestions.

Feasting the Gods at Raven Hammer Hall

Autumn has come; there's a nip in the air, and the hillsides flare with bursts of red and gold. It's a season for giving thanks and gathering in the harvest, a time to tell tales of past and present and years to come. Raven Hammer kindred is getting ready to celebrate the Winter Nights feast in honor of the ancestors and the gods.

Now before we go any further, you need to know that Raven Hammer is an imaginary group. Those of you who have already encountered the heathen community may feel you recognize some of the people in this story, but I assure you that both the kindred and its members are fiction—but a fiction that is a collage of characteristics and practices from the many kindreds and heathens I have known. So although you will not find this group, its members, or the exact practices described here anywhere, almost everything I have to say about them exists or has existed somewhere.

Let's start with the name. Although I don't know of any group called Raven Hammer, roughly 50 percent of heathen kindreds have "raven" or "hammer" somewhere in their name. The name of my own kindred, Hrafnar, means "the Ravens" in Old Norse. The ravens are Hugin and Munin, the birds who range the world to bring information to the god Odin. The Hammer is the weapon Thor uses to defend our world from the forces of destruction.

So here we are at Raven Hammer Hall. Well actually, it's a rambling ranch-style house belonging to the gothi (priest) and gythja (priestess), Thorolf and Janet, set on a two-acre lot at the edge of town. They bought the place because it has a recreation room large enough for twenty people to sit down. When they moved in, they carried fire around the boundaries of the property to claim it, explored the woods until they found the place where the forces of nature felt strongest, and made offerings to the spirits there.

Thorolf is a vice principal in the local high school, who uses a Norse name for religious activities because his region is rather conservative, and if he were known to be a heathen he could be forced out of his job. Janet is a computer programmer and uses her birth name in the heathen community and in ordinary life. They started the kindred five years ago with their two children and a friend. Now they have nine full members and four who are in training, and at every meeting, someone brings a friend.

It is Saturday afternoon, and the house is already full. Some people got in late last night and bedded down in sleeping bags in the recreation room, others have been arriving at intervals all day. Children are playing in the yard, assisted by two frenetic dogs. From the kitchen the scent of roasting pork makes mouths water. The counters are covered with food brought by members of the kindred. Those who can't bring anything put a little cash into the cookie jar. Others set up long tables in a U-shape and cover them with tablecloths the same red as the kindred banner that hangs on the wall, and people set out their feasting gear: wooden plates and bowls and decorated drinking horns. The walls are covered with hangings embroidered by Janet that portray the gods, and the mantelpiece is decorated with sheafs of wheat, gourds, and autumn flowers.

As the sun dips behind the woods, Thorolf blows a summons on a cowhorn. Fortunately, he used to play the trumpet, so it actually sounds like a horn. He has some friends who were visited by the local cops when neighbors who heard an amateur's painful squawkings thought those weirdos down the street were performing a Satanic sacrifice.

Everyone gathers in the backyard, some wearing Norse-style tunics, while for others ceremonial dress is a T-shirt with the logo of a heathen festival. Many, both men and women, wear belts with knives or swords. The kitchen door opens and Janet comes out, dressed in a blue hanging skirt (an overgarment rather like a jumper) over a white gown. Oval brooches pin the straps, and the amber necklaces she is wearing glow golden in the light of the setting sun. She holds a large drinking horn full of home-brewed mead. Her daughter, Sigrid, carries a pitcher of milk, and little Eric, a platter with a small loaf of bread.

The others fall in behind them as they take the path around the play area to the Vé. This is a long hollow surrounded by trees. At its end, a particularly fine ash tree shades the altar of heaped stone. In summer, the kindred often holds its ceremonies here, but whatever the season, this is where they begin.

Sigrid and Eric go to the ash tree, where a hollow between two roots seems to lead into the underworld. Beside it is a weathered statuette of a garden gnome. Very carefully, Eric sets the bread in the hollow and Sigrid pours the contents of the pitcher over it.

"Landwights, this is for you," says Sigrid. "Keep everything safe when it gets cold."

Now the procession moves around the tree toward the spring. Halfway between them rises a small mound of earth-covered stone. Both Janet and Thorolf moved here from other states, and their family cemeteries are a long way away, but they have buried pictures of honored relatives inside the mound and some of their kindred members have done so as well.

Janet tips the horn and mead pours onto the mound in a glistening stream. "Alfar and Dísir, honored ancestors, drink deep and give us your blessings."

For a few moments, everyone is still, listening as a sudden wind whispers in the leaves of the ash tree, then passes through the wood beyond. A squirrel runs halfway down the trunk, sees the humans, and scurries back into the branches, chattering.

"You tell'em, Ratatosk," murmurs Thorolf, and everyone laughs, remembering the squirrel who carries messages up and down the World Tree.

Now the wind is picking up in earnest, and it is getting cold. The group hurries back to the house, eager to put the last touches on dinner so they can sit down. A whole haunch of pork is steaming on a platter. Beside it is a big bowl of barley and mushrooms with gravy, dishes of carrots and cabbage, salads, and casseroles. A big chocolate cake sits to one side. Someone has put one of the Nordic Roots collections on the CD player, and feet are tapping.

Thorolf thanks Holy Earth for the gift of food and draws a Jera rune on it in blessing, and Janet takes a small plate of samples to the house spirit who lives in a cantaloupe-sized stone set by the hearth. Presently, the dogs will come in and take care of the offerings, along with anything else that's been dropped, but according to Ibn Fadlan, the Viking-Age Arab trader, when the town dogs came out to eat the offerings left by the Rus traders, the Vikings rejoiced that the food had been received by the gods, so there's precedent.

Table by table, people fill their plates and sit down. For a time, they are too busy eating to say much, but presently plates are pushed aside and the murmur of conversation grows. Maureen's mother is in the hospital. Roderic has just lost his job. There's a scandal in another kindred, and everyone wants to know what's going on. Parents collect their offspring and take them to the children's room to play. They'll take turns supervising throughout the evening.

But gradually, the room grows still. It is time for the sumble ceremony. Thorolf and Janet have moved a smaller table forward and set out the big kindred drinking horn and several bottles of beer and mead. Next to them sits a short-handled iron hammer, the big silver oath ring, a sprig of ash leaves, and the offering bowl, which was a salad bowl until Thorolf decorated it with an inscription in runes.

Thorolf moves to the center of the room and faces north, raising the hammer to begin the hallowing rite created by Edred Thorsson:

"Hammer in the north, hallow and hold this holy stead."

And so we begin . . .

Heroes and Ancestors

CHAPTER I

Before History: The First Heathens

"*Tonight,*" *Janet picks up the drinking horn and turns to face the others,* "*we have gathered here to welcome in the winter. Usually, we begin our sumble with a round for the gods and goddesses, but this feast is holy to the ancestors. I would like to propose that tonight we start by honoring our forefathers and mothers of the flesh and spirit instead.*"

She looks around the circle, listening to the murmur of agreement, and turns back to her husband. As she holds the horn, he fills it with beer, dark as the ancestral soil and foamy as the sea. It is from a batch the kindred brewed earlier that summer, and it came out very well.

Janet lifts the horn high. "*Holy ones, Alfar and Dísir, for you this drink is poured. As many grains and many drops of water mingled to make this beer, though we are the offspring of many ancestors we are one in spirit. I sign this horn with the rune Othala in token of our heritage.*" *Cradling the horn in one arm, she draws the rune in the foam.*

Karen comes up to the table. A biology major at the nearby university, she is the newest member of the kindred, and as such has the honor of serving as valkyrie. Carefully, she carries the horn to Maureen, who is sitting at the end of the table, sets it into her hands, and steps back.

"*Some of you know that I recently sent a DNA sample to England to be tested—*" *Maureen looks into the horn to see if the head has subsided enough for her to actually get a sip of beer.* "*Anyway, I got the results back last week, and I am descended from a woman who lived on the Continent around 30,000 years ago. Well, probably some of the rest of you are too," she grins, "so I hail you as cousins. Anyway, I'd like to raise this horn in honor of the woman the people at Oxford call Helena. I imagine her tending her fire, wondering if there will be enough food for her family just as I am worrying now, and I thank her for having the courage to keep going. Hailsa!" Carefully she drinks.*

"Hail Helena," the others echo as she hands the horn back to Karen and sits down.

How old is the "Old Religion"? Although heathens draw most of their religious practices from material written down during Anglo-Saxon and Viking times, those beliefs are based on millennia of evolving folk tradition. Archaeology identifies a succession of European cultures; however, recent genetic studies (see Sykes 2001) demonstrate that despite cultural changes, the population of Europe has remained remarkably stable from the Stone Age to the present day. For a comprehensive account of their migrations, see *Ancestral Journeys, the Peopling of Europe from the First Venturers to the Vikings* by Jean Manco (Thames & Hudson 2013). Honoring the ancestors, especially the *dísir,* the foremothers who guard the family line, is a core belief of Ásatrú. The "Venus" figures, which are our first evidence that humans worshipped Spirit as manifest in human form, were found in places like Uhlendorff and the Volgerherd cave in what is now Germany. Through our European grandmothers and their grandmothers who came out of Africa, and the single "African Eve" to whom all modern humans trace their origin, we are all kin.

The Stone Age

As the ice receded, human groups moved northward, settling the southern parts of Scandinavia by the year 9000 before the common era (B.C.E.). During this early period, culture and technology appear to have been similar across Europe. Our first grandmothers and grandfathers were hunter-gatherers whose religious practices included elements still found in shamanic cultures today. Living close to nature, they learned to reverence the primal beings who survived in Germanic mythology as the *jotnar* or *etins*—the giant-kin—and seek power from the animals, trees, and herbs. Scandinavian rock paintings show that predators like the wolf, bear, eagle, and raven, and strong and sometimes dangerous game animals, including the elk, aurochs, horse, and swan, had became totems that survived through the millennia as name elements, family symbols, and figures in legend. Birch, oak, ash, yew, and thorn, the sacred trees that gave their names to some of the runes, were among the trees that populated the land.

Each summer the first Scandinavians migrated from their sheltered winter camps in the lowlands to the mountains, a pattern that survived when they became a culture of cattle-herders, and remains the basis for the heathen ritual year. However, weapons found in graves suggest that both men and women also continued to hunt. An abundance of natural resources delayed the adoption of agriculture in the north until the third millennium B.C.E.

By the end of the Neolithic period, the ancestors of the Germanic peoples were living in villages and creating enduring tombs for their dead from great stones. The mounds heaped above the graves of leaders suggest that the cult of the *alfar*, or male ancestors, had become a part of the religion. The dead remained an important part of the community. Although grave finds show more gender-differentiation than was present earlier, women clearly had a high status that they retained through the Viking Age. However, there is no conclusive evidence for worship of a single "Great Goddess."

Transition to an agricultural lifestyle had other implications for religious practice. Staying in one place required people to maintain a working relationship with the spirits of the land. Village wise folk were evolving from shamans to priests who knew the rites and served the holy places. At this time, the powers being worshipped may have included a goddess of earth and water and a god of the sky, as well as the myriad spirits of field, forest, and stream.

Petroglyphs, circles, and alignments of stone were also created for ritual purposes. Although English speakers are most familiar with the megalithic monuments of the British Isles (which were there long before the Druids came), they are found all over the world, including on the European continent and in Scandinavia. Scandinavian rock art includes symbols that remained important into the Viking Age (see Gelling and Davidson, 1969). European heathens, like other contemporary pagans, perform rituals and make offerings at megalithic sites today.

Much of our evidence for early religious beliefs comes from offerings preserved in peat bogs. These include large chunks of amber that may have come from necklaces offered to local goddesses. Amber was also carved into animal images and small amulets of double-headed axes similar in form to the Thor's hammers of the Viking Age. Finely carved stone axes were also offered. Elk heads were carved on ritual items, and the wild boar was considered a great protective power. There is evidence for the sacrifice of animals, and sometimes of men. Then, as later, pots and other gifts were often ceremonially "killed" by breaking them before throwing them into the bog.

The Indo-Europeans

Sometime during the third millennium B.C.E., a new culture arrived in northern Europe, brought by the people we call the Indo-Europeans because their language was the ancestor of tongues now spoken from Brittany to Bangladesh. Although in some areas the newcomers may have replaced or displaced the earlier population, in most of Europe the major changes seem to have been technological and linguistic rather than genetic. Innovations included the ox-drawn wagon, the polished stone battle-ax, and a style of pottery known as corded ware. Our understanding of this new culture is based primarily on linguistic analysis, which has allowed philologists to reconstruct the Proto-Indo-European (PIE) language. Its vocabulary tells us what animals, plants, and tools those who spoke it knew and valued. Comparison of the myths and legends of the peoples speaking Indo-European languages offers clues to the ancestral form of the European pagan religions as well. Based on a 2013 poll, Schnurbein (2016) estimated the global heathen population as around 20,000. See also *The Horse, the Wheel and Language* by David W. Anthony (Princeton University Press, 2007).

The original Indo-European homeland was somewhere in Central Asia. Peoples who originated among the farming cultures of Anatolia may have dispersed north to the area above the Black Sea, becoming the culture known as the Kurgans, and from there moved westward. They seem to have spread out in several waves of migration. Cultural elements spread through diffusion; however, legends in which a warrior band subjugates and rules a larger population are found all across the Indo-European area. Most probably, the process was repeated again and again, as the previous conquerors became assimilated into the native population. Eventually, Proto-Indo-European split into two language groups, one in which PIE "k" sounds were retained (the *centem* languages, after the word for "one hundred" in Latin) and one in which "k" turned to "s" (the *satem* languages, after the word for "one hundred" in Old Persian). In Europe, the culture diverged into a southern and a northern branch—the "Corded-Ware" culture, from which descended the Teutons, Celts, Balts, and Slavs.

The PIE vocabulary tells us a great deal about how those who spoke it lived. It includes words for most of the familiar European animals and trees and for domesticated animals such as cows, sheep, horses, pigs, and dogs, as well as terms for the cultivation of land. The Indo Europeans farmed wheat, barley, beans, peas, and lentils, but the economic base was their herds of cows. In both the Romance and Germanic languages, the word for *cow* became the root for terms having to do with wealth, and the first warfare was the cattle raid. However, the Germanic languages include a certain percentage of

Deities of the earth included a god of the waters beneath the earth who was also the ancestor of fire, and the Moisture Mother, the goddess of the life-giving earth. Her name provided the root word that eventually evolved into our word for *humanity*. She survived as the goddess Danu from whom the Danube and many other European rivers derive their names, and the names of groups such as the Danaans, the Tuatha De Danaan, and the Danes. The moon god measured out time, and the goddess of death covered all. Other figures included a being called "Third," who fought a serpent to recover his stolen cattle, and a ferryman of the dead. Another myth that goes back to very early times is that of the cataclysmic battle between the forces of order and chaos that will end the age.

The Bronze Age

In the beginning of the *Younger Edda,* Snorri Sturlusson tells us that Odin was a descendant of King Priam of Troy, and in his *Heimskringla* (Lives of the Norse Kings), he states that the gods were called Aesir because they came from Asia. Although Snorri was an enthusiastic Norseman, he seems to have succumbed to the temptations of medieval etymological theory and the early medieval fashion for attributing national origins to the Trojans. But as we have seen, the ancestors of the present-day Scandinavians have been there for a very long time indeed. Did a small group carry the heroic culture of the Bronze Age north from the Black Sea area during the warmer years of that age, or did Germanic culture originate in Scandinavia, from which it moved south and westward during the Migrations period? There is a sense in which both theories are correct. Whether or not a significant number of people ever migrated north from Asia, some southern myths and concepts could well have been carried to Scandinavia from the Mediterranean world, where they evolved into a unique culture.

In any case, by the second millennium B.C.E., Indo-European

and native cultures had fused and were being transformed by the adoption of bronze for tools and weapons. Although their languages were beginning to differentiate, the lifestyles and beliefs of groups across northern Europe still show great similarities. Most people in the north lived in large family groups in long timber houses with outbuildings for weaving and other crafts. Families lived by mixed farming and herding. Although by this time some of the woodlands had been cleared for pasture, much of northern Europe was still thickly forested. Also, the climate was somewhat warmer than it is now, thereby supporting crops that in later times could only be grown farther south.

The land was traversed by trails. Copper, gold, tin, and amber were traded across Europe, and luxury items such as wine and jewelry were carried northward from the Mediterranean. Our most vivid portrait of life in a Bronze Age chieftain's hall can be found in the pages of the *Iliad* and the *Odyssey*. Similarities between social and political structures seen there and descriptions in later northern European epics such as *Beowulf* suggest that if allowances are made for weather and wealth, the culture of Bronze Age Germans and Scandinavians was much like Greek culture in the heroic age. For that matter, one finds the same structures and warrior traditions in the hero tales of Ireland and the epics of the Rajputs of northern India.

Where the fertility of the land could support enough people, kings and subkings ruled over territories populated by interlinked clans and families. A royal household included the warriors of the house guard, but even kings were not above taking a turn in the fields at harvest time. Warfare was a matter of raids or formal battles in which heroes fought with sword, shield, and spear and their deeds were celebrated by the bards. As later in Iceland, it was the responsibility of the ruler to make offerings to the tribal gods. The increasing importance of such leaders is shown by the rich funeral goods found in their mound-covered graves.

There is some evidence for the existence of a class of trained priests who kept the calendar and supervised the rituals. Although its authenticity has been challenged, a bronze disc found near Nebra, Germany, and dated 1600 B.C.E., shows the sun, moon and stars, suggesting a sophisticated understanding of celestial movements. This is the oldest astronomical representation yet found. It would have enabled a viewer standing on Mittelburg Hill to predict the position of the sun in relation to the Brocken—a sacred mountain where according to Jacob Grimm's *Teutonic Mythology* (1844) later folklore told of the revels of spirits and witches—and thus calculate times for planting and other agricultural tasks. The area of the Brocken seems to have been a major cultural and political center. Discoveries such as these are leading researchers to reevaluate the achievements of the Bronze Age cultures of Central Europe.

In Scandinavia, most of our information comes from petroglyphs at sites near the sea. The rock carvings show processions and rituals featuring ships and their terrestrial equivalent, the wagon, phallic men with shield and spear or double-headed ax (possibly precursors of Thor), acrobats, and couples making the sacred marriage. Bronze figures have also been found showing warriors with ritual horned helmets and dancers in short string skirts. A female figure with golden eyes may represent a forerunner of the goddess Freyja. A beautifully crafted horse and wagon holding a gilded sun disc bear witness to a solar cult that endured in Northern religious practice, if not in the mythology. Images of ploughs may portray spring ceremonies. A petroglyph of a bare footprint could be interpreted as an early symbol of the god Njordh. Also found are the long, curving horns called lurs, whose music, rising above the beat of drums and rattles, would have resounded for miles.

An interesting, if much debated, theory holds that during the earlier part of the Bronze Age a "northern Atlantis" developed on islands off the west coast of Jutland that were known as the Electrides, or Amber Isles (Spanuth 1979), dominating the lands around the North Sea until it was swamped by a tsunami somewhere between 1500 and 1220 B.C.E. Some speculate that its people were the Haunebu, who traded amber to the Egyptians. After the disaster, the fleeing inhabi-

CHAPTER TWO

Barbarians at the Gates: The Great Migrations

The horn has come to Roderic, a heavy-set man with dark hair who just turned thirty-five. His parents called him Rodrigo, but he has returned to the Visigothic form of his name. He takes the drinking horn and clears his throat.

"This seems as good a time as any to tell you all that I've got a new job," *he pauses as people cheer.* "That's the good news. The bad news is that it is in California, so I won't be here with you next year."

He waits out the murmur of dismay, and one warning to watch out, they're all weirdos out there.

"I really love it here, and I don't want to leave, but I have to go where the work is. Suddenly, I have a lot of sympathy for the Goths—I mean the real ones—" *he adds as a young man with crimson streaks in his dyed black hair and several piercings grins at him,* "and the Franks and the Saxons and all those tribes who had to leave their lands and find new homes.

"So I lift this horn to Hengest and Theodoric and all the people who followed them. May they show me how to put down roots in a new place, like they did so long ago."

Peoples in Motion

During the first millennium B.C.E., the weather began to chill, and lands that had been productive could no longer support Bronze Age levels of population. No matter where they had originally come from, northern peoples headed for warmer climates and thus into recorded history, displacing other groups in a domino effect that eventually brought them into conflict with the nations that had grown up around the Mediterranean Sea. Between the first and sixth centuries of the Common Era (C.E.), the Germanic tribes were in motion. By the time the migrations ended, the nations of modern Europe had been born.

By 500 B.C.E., the First Sound Shift (also known as Grimm's Law) had changed the sounds of the languages spoken by the peoples of Europe to create distinct tongues. During the latter half of that millennium, the first identifiably Celtic tribes were spreading out in all directions from their homeland in southern Germany/Switzerland, giving this period the name of Celtic Iron Age. Their attack on Rome in 390 B.C.E. left that nation with an enduring paranoia about fair-haired barbarians that led them to seek protection through a succession of conquests and eventually brought them up against the German tribes on the Rhine. The wealthy Celts traded with the nations of the Mediterranean, built massive hill forts, and developed elegant artistic styles.

The Germans were not so lucky. During this period, the Germanic tribes mostly stayed on their ancestral lands, initially dependent on the Celts for the iron that enabled them to plough the heavy soils. The climate was changing, and the land could no longer support them as bountifully as before. Colder winters required them to slaughter more of their livestock in the fall and keep those that remained in one half of the longhouses while the people lived in the other. But with iron ploughshares they could cultivate the same fields for longer, leading to more stable communities.

A subsistence-level culture could not support the aristocratic centers found in Celtic lands. Many Germanic terms relating to royal courts are Celtic loan words, but in the early Iron Age Germanic societies appear to have been more egalitarian than those of their Celtic neighbors. Although there were many variations in political structure, broadly speaking, tribes consisted of those who recognized the leadership of a royal clan and who, when its leader moved, followed him. The power of the tribe rested in the free men who headed households and who met in seasonal assemblies to deal with legal problems and advise the king. Kings and chieftains were supported by their house guard, who served as a first-response force in case of trouble. When the tribes began their migrations, the need for central coordination and defense increased the power of the kings.

The Germans Enter History

Our first written record of the Germanic peoples comes from the merchant and explorer Pytheas of Massilia, who journeyed to the Amber Isles around 320 B.C.E. His notes survive only as quotations in the work of later authors, but he appears to have sailed around Britain and spoken with people who had traveled to the Arctic. To many, his tales sounded too fantastic for belief. It was not until 113 B.C.E., when a Germanic tribe called the Teutones arrived in southern Gaul in company with two Celtic tribes that the Romans realized that the northlands held people who were even bigger, blonder, and scarier than the Celts of Gaul. After destroying two Roman armies, the invaders were eventually defeated, but it was clear that Rome would need to pay more attention to the north from now on.

In the middle of the first century B.C.E., Julius Caesar became proconsul for Gaul and began a campaign against the Helvetians, a tribe from what is now Switzerland who were threatening southern Gaul. In the years that followed, he battered the Celtic tribes of Gaul into submission. His encounters with the tribes to the east were less conclusive, and the river Rhine became the new Roman frontier.

Caesar identified the tribes on the west side of the river as Celts and
on the east side as Germans. But it is more probable that there was an
intermediate zone in which the two cultures mingled.

In the centuries that followed, defending the German frontier became a major concern for Rome, as seen in the battle with which the
film *Gladiator* begins. The Germans never did know when they were
beaten, and although for a time the border was pushed eastward,
eventually the Romans had to retreat to the Rhine once more. Our
most useful source for the beginning of this period is the *Germania*
of Tacitus, who served as a Roman official on the frontier. Although
much of his data was acquired secondhand, and his interpretations
are colored by a perception of the barbarians as "noble savages," the
Germania is an invaluable source of information on the nature, location, and customs of the first-century Germanic tribes. It is from
Tacitus, for instance, that we know of the goddess Nerthus and a
procession of the deity who is carried in the wagon to bless the spring
planting, whose parallel was described a thousand years later in Sweden. And it is from his writings that we know how the Romans saw
the deities being worshipped by the Continental Germans, identify-
ing Tiwaz with the Roman Mars, Wodan with Mercury, Donar with
Jupiter, and Frigg with Venus.

Although the German border could never be said to have been
completely peaceful, during the first century a conflict occurred
which left a lasting impression in Germanic legend. In 9 C.E., during
the reign of Caesar Augustus, a German chieftain of the Cherusci
tribe called Arminius, or as he is known in Germany, Hermann, rose
against them. Having served for a time as a Roman officer, he understood how to attack them. He lured three Roman legions into the
forests of the Teutoburger Wald and ambushed them there. The Roman
general Publius Varus committed suicide to avoid capture. The common soldiers were simply slaughtered, while the officers were hanged
as sacrifices. Because of this defeat, Rome ended its attempt to con-
trol northern Germany and withdrew its troops to the western bank
of the Rhine.

In the centuries that followed, relations between the western Germanic tribes and Rome followed a pattern of alternating alliance and warfare. As more Germanic warriors served in Roman armies and were stationed all over the empire, the peoples near the Rhine became more Romanized and the tribes adopted elements of Roman culture. The archaeology of the Romano-German frontier gives us a great deal of information on local belief in the form of votive altars to such powers as the Matronae (the guardian mothers) and various local deities. A temple to Mercurius Augustus (presumably a Romanized version of Wodan) stood on the site occupied by the present-day cathedral at Cologne.

The Great Migrations

For a time, the two cultures existed in equilibrium, but by the fifth century, displacements that had begun long before brought a new group of tribes into conflict with the empire. Goths from southern Sweden moved southward, scooping up Slavs and Scythians as they passed until they dominated the area from eastern Germany to the Black Sea. The Vandals, possibly originating in the Vendel area of northern Jutland, moved east and then south, gathering many peoples into an alliance that eventually followed the Danube west to the Rhine. The Burgunds seem to have taken a similar route from the Baltic coast. They might have stayed there if pressure from incoming warriors of the steppes had not forced them westward, toward the borders of Rome.

In 375, the Huns fell upon the Goths in the Ukraine. Their defeated king, Ermanarik, committed suicide, perhaps as an act of self-sacrifice. If so, it was not successful, and the fleeing Goths divided into two groups that became the Visigoths and Ostrogoths. The former eventually got as far as southern France and then Spain, while the latter fought against the Eastern Roman Empire and then the West, ending up in Italy. Italy was also the eventual home of the Langobards, who gave their name to Lombardy, while the Vandals ended up in northern Africa. From the beginning of the fifth century on, incoming tribes first fought and then became the allies of Rome, defending the borders against the next wave of invading barbarians.

The Saxon Shore

The fifth and sixth centuries were an exceptionally fertile period for the formation of legends. When the empire's troubles required that the last of the legions be withdrawn from Britain, the clash between the peoples who invaded from northern Germany and the Romano-Celtic defenders gave rise to the story of King Arthur. In the first full version of the story, written by Geoffroy of Monmouth in the twelfth century, a British magnate called Vortigern hires Saxons under a leader called Hengest to protect Britain against the raids of the Scots and Picts. When the British refuse to pay their mercenaries, Hengest calls in the rest of his tribe from across the sea. The Venerable Bede's *Ecclesiastical History of the English People* tells how Angles, Saxons, Jutes, and Frisians fought the British and each other, establishing kingdoms that remained heathen for another 200 years and retained their Germanic language even after becoming Christian.

English place names that include names such as Tiw, Thunor, Woden, and Frig show that the migrating Anglo-Saxons brought their gods with them. The English maintained close ties with the peoples of their old homelands; this explains how *Beowulf,* which takes place in Denmark, survived as the greatest work of Anglo-Saxon poetry.

From Gaul to France

The people known as the Franks, or "free," originated in the area of the middle Rhine, perhaps as an amalgamation of smaller tribes.

For a long time they lived close enough to the Romans to assimilate a great deal of their culture, and many Franks rose to high rank in the Roman armies. In the mid-fifth century, they grew more aggressive, and the Merovingian kings began to claim the territories that they had formerly defended. The greatest gains were made by King Clovis, who also converted to Christianity. By the middle of the sixth century, the Franks ruled all of Gaul, balancing Roman and Germanic elements to create an enduring fusion.

In the years that followed, the Frankish rulers supported the efforts of Irish and Anglo-Saxon missionaries to convert the peoples who lived along the North Sea, appreciating, like many other Germanic kings, the support that a unified, bureacratic church could provide to a monarchy. When the Carolingian dynasty replaced the Merovingians in the eighth century, the process of conquest and conversion continued with even greater vigor. Charlemagne pressed eastward, overwhelming the heathen tribes who had stayed in Germania, knocking out those who resisted and then forceably baptizing them and making the air ring with the sound of axes cutting down the law trees and sacred groves.

A Gathering of Heroes

By the beginning of the ninth century, the practice of heathen religion had been suppressed throughout the Germanic lands on the Continent and in the British Isles. But the mighty names of heroes such as Ermanarik, Siegfried, Theodoric, Beowulf, Hengest, Wayland, and Waltharius survived to lay a groundwork for a native European literature, as did the heroic ideals of the warrior and the tradition of loyalty that became the basis of the feudal contract between knight and lord.

The stories of the heroes who lived during the Age of Migrations passed into legend, and from legend became the stuff of popular ballads that were sung throughout the Middle Ages and have survived in remote areas like the Faeroe Islands to this day. Legends reveal the minds and hearts of the people who preserved them. By studying the old tales, we learn what the early heathens valued. By continuing to honor the heroes, we create a link with our cultural ancestors and bring their might into our own lives.

BEOWULF

The story of Beowulf, a prince from southern Sweden and eventually king of Denmark, was written down sometime between the eighth and tenth centuries, but includes historical figures dating its events somewhere in the early sixth, about the time of King Arthur. Like that story, its content belongs to the Age of Legend.

In the first part of the epic, a monster called Grendel has been attacking the hall of King Hrothgar of Denmark. Beowulf comes to help, and in single combat kills first Grendel and then his even more monstrous mother. This story inspired the second half of the film *The Thirteenth Warrior,* and as of 2006 is the subject of two more films. A second section picks up the story when Beowulf, now an old man, has himself been king of Denmark for many years. When a dragon ravages the land, only the king and one brave follower are willing to confront him, and Beowulf wins a heroic death after defeating his foe.

WAYLAND

The story of Weland (Old Norse Volundr, modern Wayland) is in some ways the most archaic of the hero tales. Indeed, it is not clear whether he should be considered human, a dwarf, or a demigod. He is mentioned in *Beowulf* and in *Thidreks Saga.* A fuller reference to his story occurs in the Anglo-Saxon poem "Deor," and in the "Lay of Volundr," one of the oldest poems in the *Poetic,* or *Elder Edda* (a collection of poems about the gods and heroes written down around 1200). The story tells how the great smith Weland is captured by King Nithard, hamstrung to keep him from escaping, and forced to create mighty works for his captor. He takes his revenge by killing the king's sons and impregnating his daughter, then, like Daedalus, escapes on the magical wings he has crafted while a prisoner.

SIEGFRIED

The interaction between the Huns and the Burgunds gave rise to the greatest of Germanic legends, the story of Siegfried (Old Norse, Sigurd) and the treasure of the Nibelungs. Like the story of King Arthur in Britain, it is based on a historical incident, in this case the massacre of the Burgund royal house by the Huns in 437. Around this kernel the greatest legends of the Germanic peoples accreted to become the story preserved in the German *Nibelungenlied,* the Norse *Volsungasaga,* and eventually Richard Wagner's great operas. The first half of the story is the tale of the young hero Siegfried/Sigurd who wins a magic ring and a great treasure from a dragon and becomes the lover of the valkyrie Brunhild, but is then enchanted by the magic of the Burgund queen to forget Brunhild and marry her daughter Kriemhild/Gudrun, only to be killed by the greedy Burgund kings. In the second part, Gudrun is married off to Attila, the great king of the Huns, who eventually avenges Siegfried by murdering Gudrun's brothers, while the ring and the gold end up in the Rhine.

This story is preserved in two major works and numerous poems and ballads. The oldest reference to the legend is a passage in *Beowulf.* Other versions can be found among the heroic lays collected in the *Elder Edda,* which includes poems about a number of the more important episodes. Particularly interesting is the "Lay of Sigdrifa," in which Sigurd awakens the valkryie (in other Old Norse sources called Brynhild). She greets the world in one of our oldest heathen prayers. This passage was also used by Wagner in the scene in the opera *Siegfried* in which he awakens Brunhild. These lays provided the basis for the prose *Volsungasaga,* a multigenerational family saga that begins with the origin of the family line from the god Odin and gathers together all the elements of the story into a single tale. Although it was written down after the *Nibelungenlied* (sometime

during the thirteenth century), the society of Iceland preserved archaic cultural elements that make the saga feel older.

The *Nibelungenlied* was composed at about the same time that the
lays of the *Elder Edda* were being written down, but it comes from a
very different world. The Germany of the thirteenth century belonged fully to medieval Christendom. In this version, most of the
heroic trappings have been replaced by Christian elements—for instance, Brunhild and Kriemhild quarrel over the ring on the church
steps—but the essential power of the tale remains.

From there, the story passed into folklore, and the heroes of the
Rhine continued to be celebrated in Scandinavian songs. The danced
"kvaedhi" of the Faeroe Islands includes a particularly rich trove, in
which incidents from the *Volsungasaga* are retold.

THEODORIC

A hero who is almost certainly based on a historical character is
Theodoric. It is probably this Theodoric, a sixth-century Gothic
ruler who ruled Italy from Ravenna, where his magnificent tomb remains, who is mentioned in the Old English poem "Deor." A version
of his story is preserved in *Thidreks Saga,* and in the medieval German *Dietrich of Bern.* However, he was also inserted into the *Nibelungenlied,* a century before his true time, as a Gothic warrior in
the following of Attila.

CHAPTER 3

From Vikings to Vinland

Now the drinking horn comes to Freydis, a young woman wearing a pleated shift and hanging skirt in the style of the Swedish Viking town of Birka that expands nicely to accommodate the child she is expecting any day.

"I suppose I ought to be hailing all the Viking women who gave birth in sod houses with blizzards howling around the eaves," Freydis grins. "But instead I want to honor Queen Sigrid, sometimes called the Haughty. I would rather call her a woman who knew her own worth and her own mind. She was married first to the old king of Sweden, and when she found out the Swedes expected her to commit suttee when he died, decided she didn't love him that much, and left." She waits for the laughter to subside.

"When she got home, Olaf Tryggvason of Norway decided she would be a suitable wife and came courting. Things were going fine until he told her he expected her to convert to Christianity. She said she had no problem with him worshipping whatever gods pleased him, but she was going to stick with the gods of her ancestors, thank you. At that point he called her a 'heathen bitch' and slapped her, and that was the end of that engagement. She married the king of Denmark instead and supported the coalition that finally brought King Olaf down.

"So here's to you, Sigrid!" she lifts the horn. "So far as I know I'm not your descendant, but if you'd like to send some of your spirit to this

daughter I'm carrying, I'd welcome you! Hailsa!" She dips her finger into the beer and dabs some on her forehead and then on her belly and gives the horn back to the valkyrie.

Raiders and Traders

In Europe, the years between the fall of the Roman Empire and the emergence of medieval culture are known as the Dark Ages. But while the holy steads of Germania burned, in Scandinavia the troth of the old gods was alive and well. Protected by distance, change came gradually to the north, giving workers in metal and wood the time to develop distinctive artistic styles worthy to stand with the greatest achievements of the Mediterranean. Among them are the exquisite gold bracteates that feature our oldest images of the gods. Amulets and helmet plates show totemic beasts and acts of worship. In the north, the fashion for interlace that had originated among the Copts of Egypt developed into an exuberant concatenation of artistic elements in which the spiritual interpenetrates the physical world.

Between the fifth and ninth centuries, Scandinavia prospered. Chieftains expanded their territory to become kings, and the population grew. As pressure on space and resources increased, a people who had maintained their warrior tradition began to eye the rich lands to the south. A hundred years after the English had abandoned their faith for the new religion, its shadow side rose up against them as the last of the unconverted Germanic peoples attacked the monastery at Lindisfarne. The century that followed saw an unprecedented explosion of energy as Norse raiders and traders took off in all directions, coursing the seas in their exquisitely engineered dragon ships.

It should be pointed out that at no time did *all* the Norse go a-viking. But funding a ship and crew was a good way to occupy fractious younger sons for the summer while the heirs to steadings stayed home and got on with the farming. With their shallow draft, the Viking ships could sail up rivers to sack cities well inland. At first, the Vikings were after loot, but soon they realized that the real wealth of the south was in land. The first and easiest pickings were in England. Successive raids from Denmark and Norway were so successful that many Danish warriors married local girls and took up farms or went back home to get their families.

By the end of the ninth century, Britain was partitioned between the English and Danes. The northeastern area became known as the Danelaw, and the city of York became the Norse town of Jorvik, the capital of a Scandinavian kingdom that lasted for another hundred years. The Viking Museum in York includes a reconstruction of parts of the old Viking town on the site of the excavations.

In the eleventh century, King Canute married the English queen Emma and ruled a Scandinavian empire that included England, Denmark, and Norway. Vikings from Norway raided and later settled the northern coasts of Scotland and the Shetland and Orkney Isles, as well as the Faeroes, which are equidistant from Britain, Norway, and Iceland. We who are accustomed to looking at maps whose center is the equator may find it hard to realize how strategically important the Vikings found these islands, which served as bases and way stations from which they could move in any direction. Viking raids on Ireland were followed by the creation of a kingdom, whose capital was the ancestor of modern Dublin. Like York, Dublin now has a Viking museum where the results of excavations can be seen.

At the beginning of the tenth century, the province on the north coast of France was ceded to Hrolf the Ganger and his followers and was renamed Normandy. The Normans quickly assimilated the French religion and language, but in the centuries that followed the old Viking energy drove one group of Normans south to found the kingdom of Sicily and set Duke William the Bastard, the grandson of Hrolf, to conquer England.

Rus warriors from Sweden pushed eastward, rowing and portaging their ships up the rivers as they sought a route to Constantinople. Some stayed to serve in the emperor's Varangian guard, while others realized there was more money to be made as merchants than as fighters. The trading posts they established along the Volga were the first towns in Russia, the land that still bears their name. The account of a meeting with Rus traders given by the Arab trader Ibn Fadlan includes some very interesting information and was the inspiration for the first part of the film *The Thirteenth Warrior*. In all these lands, the incomers were eventually assimilated into the local cultures, contributing personal and place names and a legacy of Viking vigor.

One reason that Norsemen of spirit began to look for land elsewhere during the ninth century was the fact that at home their lords were doing their best to become absolute monarchs in the style of the rulers of Continental Europe. Like the Germanic kings before them, Scandinavian kings could see the benefits in a system in which one king under one god ruled the land. Snorri Sturlusson's *Heimskringla* (*Lives of the Norse Kings*) tells the story of the complex conflicts through which Norway became a medieval kingdom, and the cruelty with which its kings imposed Christianity.

Islands in the Western Sea

As royal pressure increased, men began to leave for a newly discovered island in the western sea called Iceland, seeking, as so many immigrants to the United States did later on, political and religious freedom. The settlement established by those first settlers developed a unique Norse culture to which we owe the treasure of lore that is the basis for modern Ásatrú.

At the time of the land-taking, the climate of Europe had warmed sufficiently to make an island just below the Arctic Circle a viable proposition. Despite its name, even today the climate of Iceland is relatively mild. Geologically, Iceland is a very young and active island, a land of fire and ice whose natural features are an obvious inspiration for the elemental imagery in Norse creation mythology. The rift where the North American and European continental plates join runs through it, the only place where they meet on dry land. When the Norse arrived, they found a country whose coastlands were rich in grass and scrub birch and whose waters were full of fish, even though the central part of the island was, and remains, a wasteland of glacier and lavaflow. The first Norsemen to arrive claimed great tracts that they later subdivided into holdings for their followers.

Our knowledge of the settlement and history of Iceland comes mainly from the sagas, prose narratives of a quality unmatched elsewhere in Europe until the Renaissance that are perhaps the greatest achievement of Scandinavian literature. Written down during the thirteenth and fourteenth centuries, they include family sagas set 200 or 300 years earlier during the period of the Icelandic republic, which is also known as the Saga Age. Other sagas (like the *Volsungasaga*) preserved the earlier Germanic tradition, chronicled the histories of the Norse kings, or presented Norse versions of European chivalric romances such as the story of Tristan and Isolde. The literature also included saints' lives and histories of events in the medieval period.

Most interesting from our point of view are the family sagas, which focus on the conflicts and activities (including the religious practices) of ordinary people. Although their authors were Christian, the process of conversion in Iceland had been gradual (see chapter 4), and they were writing about their recent ancestors. Although some incidents may have been exaggerated for dramatic effect, we can accept much of the material as authentic. Thus, heathens possess more information on the pre-Christian practice of their religion than any other reconstructed pagan tradition (except Hellenism) can claim.

The other great sources of information on heathen religion are the *Poetic*, or *Elder Edda*, and the *Edda* written by Snorri Sturlusson (also called the *Prose Edda*), a textbook for poets that summarizes the stories and analyzes the technique for writing the exceedingly complex style of poetry popular in Scandinavia during the early Middle Ages. The first historical works, the *Islendigabók* (*Book of the Icelanders*) and the *Landnamabók* (*The Book of Landtaking*), were written down in the first half of the twelfth century. Later sagas such as the *Laxdaelasaga* also provide accounts of how the first settlers arrived from Norway and took up land. When Iceland began to fill up, Erik the Red led a group of settlers to the land he called Greenland, a name that had been deliberately chosen to make it attractive. The Norse voyages to North America are described in the *Saga of Erik the Red* and *The Greenland Saga*.

The southern coasts of Greenland did have good grazing and were rich in game, and for a time the colony prospered. From Greenland, Erik's son, Leif the Lucky, led an expedition that in 1000 reached the North American coast. The exact location of the place he named Vinland is still debated, but archaeological evidence has been found for a temporary Norse settlement at L'Anse aux Meadows on the northern coast of Newfoundland. The Greenlanders continued to visit North America to cut timber for some years, but no evidence for any permanent settlement has been found. The Kensington Rune Stone found in Minnesota in 1898 is almost certainly a forgery.

Hof and Hall

In the sagas, someone who has a deep devotion to one of the gods is known as "Thorsvin" or "Freysvin"—the "friend" of Thor or Freyr. This way of referring to the relationship seems typical of the Norse attitude toward their gods. Rather than coming to the gods as manipulators or supplicants, the heathen approached his deities as an ally. This was literally true for those heroes who were taken up by Odin's valkyries to join the host in Valhalla, but there was a sense in which all gods and humans were allied in the struggle to maintain a productive order against the forces of chaos in the world.

"Professional" priests are mentioned in continental sources and as part of the royal cult at Uppsala in Sweden. It is in Sweden also that we hear of a temple of the god Freyr whose property was administered by a full-time priestess who was considered to be the "wife" of the god. However, among the West Norse and Icelanders there were no full-time clergy. In Iceland, the term *gothi* (also spelled *godhi*) refers to the most notable man of a district, to whom others swore loyalty. He represented them at the Allthing, the Icelandic institution that combined the functions of a congress and supreme court. In the heathen period, he was also responsible for making the offerings and hosting the feast at the great seasonal holy days. Those who were friends of the gods might build a shrine to the deity and act as his priest for those who had need, but they were also full-time farmers.

The hof built by Thorolf Mostersegg is described in *Eyrbyggjasaga* (chapter 4) was a large building with a door on one side. Within, the place was divided into the public area and the sanctuary, which consisted of an area like a church choir with a platform that served as an altar. Temple furniture included the oath ring, which was worn by the priest at ceremonies, and a bowl for the blood of offerings and the twig used to sprinkle it. Around this platform stood the images of the gods. Intervention by a priest was not necessary to seek the gods, nor was everyone required to honor them. In fact, some warriors preferred to trust to their own strength instead. People honored all the gods, or one, or none. For heathens, religious practice was a matter of individual choice, not community convention. Many Viking traders accepted baptism so that they could do business with Christians and found it hard to understand why the Christian priests got upset when they added an image of Jesus to the statues in the family shrine.

Devotion to a specific deity might become a family tradition. Several of the first settlers in Iceland brought carved pillars dedicated to Thor, which they cast overboard as they neared the coast so that the god could show them where he wished them to land. Jarl Hakon of Halogaland in Norway worshipped two goddesses who may have been deified ancestresses: Thorgerda Hölgabrúdh and her sister, Irpa, who aided Hakon with battle magic in time of need. Odin appears to have been the patron deity of Egil Skallagrimsson's line.

Kings and war leaders sacrificed to Odin before battle, and every-

CHAPTER 4

Conversion

Now Karen offers the horn to a blond boy whose sprouting beard looks as new as his silver Thor's hammer. He grips the horn as if afraid he'll drop it.

"Hi everyone," he stares into the horn. "My name is Cliff, and this is my first time here. I want to thank you all for letting me come." The atmosphere warms, and he dares to look up. "Andy here brought me," he nods at the young man sitting next to him. "I bumped into him in the stacks at the university library. We were both trying to find a copy of the Islendigabók in translation. I've been reading everything I could find about the Vikings and what they believed. I didn't know there was anybody else who cared about this stuff—in modern times, I mean. I just know that I can't go to my parents' church anymore. A god who wants all his worshippers to be sheep doesn't make sense to me. And when I talk to Thor I feel like someone is listening." He blushes, clears his throat, and goes on.

"But since we're honoring ancestors right now, I want to drink to the Lawspeaker of Iceland, who worked out a compromise so even though they were officially Christian, people could keep some of the old ways, which is why we have all that information I found in the library."

The *Islendigabók* is the first historical saga, written by the priest Ari the Learned. The Lawspeaker in question was a heathen called Thorgeir Thorkelsson of Ljósavatn, and the Christian leader, Sidhu-Hallr, was the man who refused to lead his coreligionists in civil war and asked Thorgeir to find a compromise that would allow Iceland to survive as a united and independent nation. Thorgeir wrapped himself in his cloak and meditated. When he emerged from his seclusion, he suggested that they preserve the peace by officially turning Christian—at least in public—but allow folk to worship as they wished when they were at home. Thus, the conversion of Iceland, which officially took place in 1000, was gradual and without bitterness. Icelanders, reknowned as the best poets in Scandinavia, continued to use the old mythology as the basis for their work, with the result that when people started to write down their lore, it was remembered. And even when people ceased to honor the gods, they continued to make offerings to the spirits of the land. Unfortunately, the great Icelandic compromise that allowed a peaceful conversion seems to have been unique in the annals of Christianity.

For the modern heathen, the question of when, how, and why those whom we might call the last "native speakers" of the old religion converted to the new one is of primary importance. Had the old gods failed them? Were they bored with the old ways? Or were there other reasons, which had little to do with the people's actual needs or desires?

Migration Age Conversion

Most of the Germanic tribes who invaded Roman lands converted first to the Arian form of the Christian religion. Theologically, the major difference seems to have been that Arianism saw Jesus as subordinate rather than coequal with God the Father. In practice, there were some differences in ritual. Arians held their services in the evening and may have had a somewhat simpler ritual. There's at least one accusation from an anti-Arian writer, Vigilius (in *Two Books against the Arian Heretic Palladius*), that the Arian priests wore neck rings and arm rings, so they may have preserved some heathen ways. To the orthodox Catholics, of course, they were heretics, and when a pagan Roman general led the empire's armies against invading Arian barbarians, the Christian bishops hardly knew which side to pray for.

ENGLAND

The Romano-British Christians who had lived in southeastern Britain were killed, enslaved, or fled before the Angles, Saxons, and Jutes, who colonized the land after the great invasions in the fifth century. During the sixth century, Celtic missionaries from Wales and Ireland attempted to spread the word among the heathens on the Continent, but left England alone. Thus, there was neither opportunity for nor pressure on the newcomers to adopt their culture and religion, and the first English kingdoms remained happily heathen, developing royal lines who traced their descent from Wodan or Ing.

The beginning of the end of Anglo-Saxon heathenism was signaled by the arrival of the missionary Augustine of Canterbury in 597. He was sent by Pope Gregory, who had apparently in his youth seen some English slave boys and dubbed them "not Angles, but angels!" The full story may be found in the *Ecclesiastical History of the English People* by the Venerable Bede. The process followed the common pattern of imposition from the top down by kings who had been brought into the Christian orbit by alliance or marriage.

The first Christians in the Roman Empire might have been slaves and the poor, but in five centuries the Church had learned that it was much more efficient to convert the rulers first and leave it to them to impose the new faith on their subjects. In England, Augustine went first to King Aethelberht of Kent, who was married to the daughter of the (Christian) Frankish King Charibert, which is why Canterbury is the senior bishopric in the Church of England to this day. Their daughter married King Edwin of Northumbria, giving the new religion a foothold in the north. It is said that Coifi, who had been the chief of the heathen priesthood, converted because many who had been less active in the service of the gods than he had nonetheless received greater rewards. We are not told whether Coifi's hopes for prosperity in his new religion were fulfilled. Nor did the new god preserve the Northumbrian king, who fell in battle against a Welsh-Mercian alliance.

However, despite setbacks the Christians were persistent, and one kingdom after another turned to the new faith. By the end of the seventh century, most of the kingdoms had permanent Christian communities and kings, who if not observant, had at least been baptized. Even King Penda of Mercia allowed his son to be baptized when he married a Christian princess. Penda freely allowed the new priests to preach their religion, but was loud in his condemnation of those who failed to practice the virtues in which they said they believed. He, too, died fighting, and although the vigor with which English bishops continued to preach against heathen customs during the following centuries suggests that conversion was not complete, Christianity had become the official religion of the British Isles.

GERMANY

Like the Visigoths and other tribes that settled within the Roman Empire, the Franks had become Christian by the early sixth century. Once their hold on Gaul was secure, they turned their attention to the subjugation of the peoples now inhabiting the lands from which they had come. Successive campaigns brought them victory in Frisia, Thuringia, and Alamannia. During the seventh century, they encouraged missionary work by Irish monks, and after the conversion of England, missionaries began to come from that country as well.

The English priests Wilfrid and Willibrord were sent to Frisia, but the form of Christianity to which they attempted to convert the natives was Frankish. Duke Radbod of Frisia agreed to take religious instruction. In the *Vita Vulframni*, we are told that when he was about to be baptized, he was told that although he himself would go to heaven, his ancestors were in hell, so he changed his mind, not wanting to be separated from them in the afterlife.

But by the eighth century the Merovingian dynasty was failing. It fell to the Carolingians who succeeded them, and in particular to Charles the Great, to impose the new religion by force on the conquered peoples. Pepin, who took the monarchy from the last of the Merovingians, was the first Frankish monarch to be crowned by Christian rites. Charlemagne took the process a step further in 800, when he was made Holy Roman Emperor by the pope.

Charlemagne's campaign against the Saxons began as a reprisal for raids across the Rhine, but it became a crusade, accomplished by fire and sword. In 772, he penetrated deeply into Saxon territory. Following the example of St. Boniface, who had cut down the oak of Donar at Geismar, he destroyed the Irminsul, the great pillar associated with the god Tyr that was the focus of Saxon spirituality and law. Conquered Saxon chieftains were baptised—if necessary, being stunned by clubs to hold them still for it. In retaliation for a Saxon raid in 782, Charlemagne massacred 4,500 prisoners at Verden, leading to even more widespread rebellion. The antiheathen edicts of the years that followed make it clear that the conquered did not give up their religion willingly.

The Conversion of Scandinavia

After his death, Charlemagne's empire began to fragment. The crusading zeal that had converted the Frisians faded before the Franks could tackle Denmark. Thus, the religious, if not the political, life of Scandinavia remained peaceful. Throughout the ninth century, churchmen prayed to be delivered from the fury of Vikings who were all the more horrifying because they were heathen. But as the Northmen began settling instead of raiding, many found it useful to take the same faith as their neighbors, and in the unsettled political climate of the tenth century, exiled Norse princes realized that conversion to the religion of the kings with whom they had taken refuge could win them support and alliance.

Denmark was the first to fall, when King Harald Bluetooth took the new religion and not only imposed it on his people but also, retroactively, on his parents, as he proclaimed in the great runestone that was erected in Jelling when he moved their remains from their mounds to the church there. In theory, Danish bishoprics existed already, but the conversion may have been intended to deprive the Germans, to whom Harald already paid tribute, of a reason to invade Denmark. Whatever Harald's reasons, men who refused to convert at his order were forced to do so.

In Norway, the long-lived and much-married King Harald Hairfair remained heathen to his death, but as his many sons squabbled over the kingship, they sometimes found Christian alliances useful. The oldest, Eric Bloodaxe, was baptized with his wife, Queen Gunnhild, during one of their periods of exile in the Viking kingdom in England. Harald's youngest son, Hakon, was fostered by King Aethelstan of England, who raised him as a Christian. Harald's great-grandson, Olaf Tryggvason, was introduced to Christianity as a young man when he took refuge in the Norse princedoms in Russia. After taking power in Norway, all these kings attempted to impose their new religion on their countrymen.

The most tolerant of these Christian kings was Hakon, the only one of Harald's sons to be called "the Good." Hakon, who was called to the throne by the heathen jarl, Sigurd of Lade, when his older brother, Eric, proved a tyrant, was indeed a good king who respected the rights of his people. When he told them they should convert to Christianity, they responded that they had thought he was bringing them freedom, but now he was attempting to:

> thrall-bind us anew in this strange wise, that we must forgo
> the faith which our fathers and all our forefathers had before
> us, first in the burning age and now in the howe age; they

were much greater than we and all the same this faith has availed us well.... [We] will all follow thee and hold thee for king as long as there is alive one of the bonders here at the thing, if thou, O king, wilt forbear with us and bid us only such things as we can give thee and which are not unmeet for us to do. ("The History of Hacon the Good," cited in Sturlusson 1990, ch. 15)

In any case, the bonders (free farmers), who had so far tolerated their king's strange ways, now required him to join them at the autumn feast instead of eating separately and nearly rebelled when he refused to eat the sacrificial horsemeat or drink to Odin from the horn. Eventually, he had to compromise by breathing in the steam from the broth in which the meat had been boiled ("Hacon," cited in Sturlusson 1990, chapter 17). Thus, Hakon kept the loyalty of his people and was able to fight off the sons of Eric for another twenty years. Though he won his last battle, he died of his wounds, and the skald Eyvind claimed him for the old faith in the poem called the "Hakonarmál," in which valkyries carry Hakon to Valhall.

The poem ends with the words:

> Wealth dies, kinsmen die,
> The land is laid waste.
> Since Hacon fared to the heathen gods
> Many are thralls and slaves. ("History of Hacon," cited in
>   Sturlusson 1990, ch. 32)

And so it proved, when Olaf Tryggvason came to power. Throughout these years, many men had allowed themselves to be baptised so that they could trade with Christian Europe, or agreed to do so when ordered by a Christian overlord. Some chieftains welcomed missionaries and built churches to encourage Christian merchants to come and trade. But Northmen were notorious for returning to their old ways.

King Olaf resolved to put an end to that. Of those who were not persuaded by threats or promises, "some he slew, some he maimed, and some he drove away from the land" ("History of Olaf Tryggvason," cited in Sturlusson 1990, ch. 53). He pillaged the heathen temples and destroyed the images of the gods. Those who were called "troll-wise" (workers of magic) he drowned or killed by setting a bowl full of hot coals on the belly. A chieftain was killed by being forced to swallow a poisonous snake.

During this period, the Christian assault on Iceland was taking place as well. Some of those who emigrated to that country were seeking to escape the political and religious aggression of the Norse kings, and missionaries had a rough time. Skalds wrote of the conflict as a battle between Christ and Thor. As described earlier, the situation was resolved by a compromise the same year Olaf Tryggvason was killed.

The third of the "converting kings" bore the nickname of "Digri," which can be translated as "the fat," "the big-mouthed," or "full of himself," although he is known to history as St. Olaf. He had been baptised as a child at the order of Olaf Tryggvason, who stood as his godfather. According to Snorri, as king:

> He investigated the Christianity of men, and when it seemed lacking to him, he made known the right customs to them, and he laid so much upon it that if there was anyone who did not wish to leave Heathenry, he drove some out of the land; some he let have their feet or hands hewn off or their eyes gouged out; some he let be hanged or hewn down, but he let no one go unpunished who did not wish to serve God. ("History of St. Olaf," cited in Sturlusson 1990, ch. 73)

Eventually, he managed to turn so many of his people (both Christian and heathen) against him that he, too, was killed. His successors found it expedient to proclaim him a saint, although during his life he had been noted for crusading zeal rather than any kind of holiness. As P. H. Sawyer puts it, the Scandinavian rulers "had discovered what great advantages Christianity could confer on kings, and only that can explain the extraordinary ferocity with which they evangelized." (1982, p. 139)

King Olaf's Land

In the years that followed, the new religion tightened its hold on the land. Churches were built on the mounds of the noble dead or on the sites of demolished pagan temples, and bishops became powers in the land. The holy feasts became saints' days, though many heathen practices were retained. The old beliefs lingered long in the countryside, and as in Iceland, the land spirits were honored even when the old gods were denied.

Just as the culture of the Mediterranean world was based on Graeco-Roman literature, Germanic mythology remained the foundation of northern culture. The days of the week continued to bear the names of the gods. To this day, personal names in Scandinavia such as Torbjorn or Saga also recall them. Even the Christianity of the North acquired a subtly heathen flavor. Scenes of Sigurd (Siegfried) killing the dragon were carved on the portals of churches, a cross from the Isle of Man shows Odin being devoured by the Wolf. A Saxon version of the gospel, the "Heliand," portrays Jesus as a king and the apostles as his warband. The old stories survived in ballads and folktales, albeit in mutated form. Stories of the Wild Hunt that rides at Yuletide are found from Germany to Norway, led by historical figures such as Dietrich of Bern, or Gudrun and Sigurd, who despite being titled "Sigurd Swain"—"Sigurd the Young"—is described as being old and half-blind. Folklore ascribing various kinds of weather to Thor or Loki was current as late as the twentieth century.

We are indebted to Snorri Sturlusson for the survival of much of the mythology. Writing two centuries after the conversion, he organized the old stories into a manual for poets. As mentioned earlier, a great deal of information about belief and practice was also included in the Icelandic sagas. In addition, Icelandic families treasured their collections of old lore. This is still true—in the 1960s, an artist I know funded a trip around Iceland by illustrating copies of the sagas at the farmhouses where he stayed.

The Catholicism of medieval Scandinavia adopted and adapted the old ways where it could not ignore them. Although the Protestant Reformation introduced a religion of greater severity, the development of national churches spurred an interest in national heritage. The fight of Arminius against the Romans described in Tacitus's *Germania*, first printed in 1472, was seen as a precursor of the struggle of the German Protestants against Rome. In England, the dissolution of the monasteries by Henry VIII made their manuscript collections available to English antiquarians.

By the seventeenth century, scholars in Denmark (which at that time ruled both Norway and Iceland), were developing an interest in Scandinavian antiquities.

At the same time as Danish officials were treating Iceland like a conquered country, the king was ordering bishops to submit reports on all monuments and other antiquities in their dioceses. Manuscripts were collected and folk songs and tales were written down. Missionaries among the Saami recorded beliefs that preserved a Norse influence. Johannes Bureus collected Swedish runic inscriptions and began the study of runelore.

Although the religion had been suppressed, the lore remained, and buried in the collective unconscious of the Germanic peoples, the old gods waited for men and women to call on them once more.

CHAPTER 5

The Roots of the Revival

The horn has come to Caroline, an athletic young woman home on leave from the U.S. Air Force. She looks around the circle and grins.

"Cliff discovered Heathenry in books. I got it from music. My parents didn't have much use for religion, but they loved opera. I grew up on the Ring *cycle—no I don't mean the* Lord of the Rings, *though I read that, too—I mean the story of Siegfried and Brunhilde. When I grew up, I wanted to be a valkyrie," she nods to Karen. "I didn't know about this kind. Anyway, listening to that music was a religious experience for me. In the music, I found a world that was full of magic and heroic deeds. You could say I came to Ásatrú through Wagner's operas, so I'd like to lift this horn in his honor!"*

Some have seen the Norse abandonment of the old ways as Ragnarök, the end of the heathen world, which was replaced by the new world of Christianity. The fourth opera in the *Ring* cycle is called *Götterdämmerung,* which can be translated as either "the Twilight" or "the Doom" of the gods. But did the gods die, or were they pushed into the "twilight" of the unconscious, waiting for us to call them back into the light of day?

The Romance of the Past

In a sense, of course, the old gods were never forgotten. However fragmentary and distorted, their names and stories survived in those lands where they had once been worshipped. But during the seventeenth and eighteenth centuries, the intelligentsia of Europe were working to create a single "enlightened" culture, as medieval thinkers had sought to make all lands part of a united Christendom. It was not until the beginning of the nineteenth century that things began to change. New social ideas challenged the old hierarchies. Individuals sought support in their quest for freedom from others who shared their own culture. The struggle for the rights of man became the fight for the rights of peoples, and emerging nations sought an identity in an idealized past.

All over Europe, scholars and romantics began to explore the folklore and legends of their native lands. In the Germanic countries, they turned from the culture of the Mediterranean world to their own. The Swedish Gotiska Förbund studied Old Norse literature and preached political reform. In Germany, Jacob and Wilhelm Grimm gathered their famous collection of fairy tales. Jacob was one of the fathers of modern philology, and in 1844 he completed his masterwork, the four-volume *Teutonic Mythology*, which traced the connections between Norse mythology and the surviving folk traditions of Germany, and remains one of the most useful sources for information on heathen religion today.

In England, publication of old ballads and the first translation of the *Poetic Edda* sparked interest in ancient Scandinavia. Edward Gibbon wrote of the Germans who fought the Roman Empire with admiration, and Thomas Carlyle's essays praised the northern heroic virtues. The poet Matthew Arnold wrote about Balder, and Algernon Swinburne about Hertha. Toward the end of the nineteenth century, the writer and artist William Morris traveled to Iceland and published his own translation of the *Volsungasaga*.

Even in the United States the song of the North was heard. Henry Wadsworth Longfellow linked the Vikings to the New World in his poem "The Skeleton in Armor" and retold a number of stories from Snorri Sturlusson's *Heimskringla* in the collection *Tales of a Wayside Inn*.

The story of Siegfried had been treated by several German poets and playwrights earlier in the nineteenth century, but the Italian tradition still dominated opera when Richard Wagner presented his monolithic music drama in 1876. Some found his new music shocking, others became enthusiastic "Wagnerites." Drawing primarily from the story as told in the *Volsungasaga*, Wagner created a new version of the legend, expressing his own ideas about society, life, and love. In Wagner's version, the Ring, which had been a minor element in the original, became a talisman that gives its owner ultimate power. But the curse of its maker brings death to all who bear it. The god Wotan (Odin), himself briefly seduced by the Ring's temptation, cannot seize it without breaking the treaties that keep order in the world. Only by creating a being—his grandson Siegfried—who is totally free, can he return the gold to the Rhinemaidens and negate its curse. By the time the valkyrie Brunhilde, who is Siegfried's beloved, finally figures out what must be done and why, the opera has thoroughly explored the conflicts between freedom and responsibility, greed and sacrifice, love and the lust for power.

In the years that followed, the valkyrie became the icon of an operatic soprano, and Siegfried the archetype of the hero, but it is Wotan, striving, conniving, and wandering the world as he seeks a way to save it, who brought back awareness of the northern gods. Modern singers have reported that performing in the *Ring* cycle is "almost like a religious experience." Long before it occurred to anyone that it might be possible to actually practice the old ways, Wagner's music was making people aware of a spiritual power very different from the faith they knew.

Blood and Soil

During the first years of the twentieth century, writers and artists like Guido "von" List (the developer of the Armanen runes) and Ludwig Fahrenkrog were creating a new mysticism based on German legend and closely tied to the land. Unfortunately, this first attempt to reconstruct the ancient religion was flawed by attempts to mix it with astrology, theosophy, and esoteric Christianity. For Germans still trying to forge a national identity from the newly united German states, the native religion provided useful symbols, but the distinction between cultural and racial identity blurred. In Germany (as well as in Britain and the United States), Charles Darwin's theories regarding the survival of the fittest had inspired, among other things, the idea that humans should use selective breeding to improve their own species as they did their animals. When this concept met the anti-Semitism inherited from medieval Christianity, it spawned a deadly ideology of racial hatred.

Here I must emphasize that racism has no basis in the lore. For the ancient Germanic peoples, the important relationship was to the immediate and extended family or clan. Beyond that stood loyalty to a king or war leader. The tribe was a collection of clans and families who followed a given leader. Whether other tribes were enemies or allies depended on whether they had common or conflicting interests, not on race, as can be seen by the treatment of Attila and the Huns in the Siegfried stories, and by the fact that the Vikings took slaves wherever they raided, irrespective of race or religion. Nationhood was a very late concept indeed. In particular, prejudice against the Jews was an outgrowth of European Christianity that never took root in Scandinavia. However it proved fatally attractive to Germans seeking a scapegoat for their sufferings after the first World War.

Much has been written about the "occult roots" of Nazism. However, their own writings indicate that although they may have adopted some heathen symbols such as the swastika, most of the Nazi leaders had no interest in anything that resembled authentic Germanic religion. Some were irreligious, some anti-Catholic, but others considered themselves good Christians. Those who like Heinrich Himmler and Karl Wiligut were interested in the occult drew their inspiration from an eclectic mish-mash of sources (Steigman-Call 2003).

It would be more correct to say that the chief deity in Nazi Germany was not Wotan, but Adolf Hitler himself. The following passage makes Hitler's opinion clear:

> What nonsense! Here we have at last reached an age that has left all mysticism behind, and now he [Himmler] wants to start that all over again. We might just as well have stayed in the church. At least it had tradition. . . . Isn't it enough that the Romans were erecting great buildings when our forefathers were still living in mud huts; now Himmler is starting to dig up these villages of mud huts and enthusing over every potsherd and stone axe he finds. All we prove by that is that we were still throwing stone hatchets and crouching around open fires when Greece and Rome had already reached the highest stage of culture. We really should do our best to keep quiet about this past.
>
> (reported by Speer 1970, pp. 94–95)

In fact, Nazi decoration and architecture make it clear that Hitler's greatest inspiration was not ancient Germany, but Imperial Rome.

Those "pagan" Germans who did not support the Nazis went to the concentration camps with the rest of the misfits. The fate of some of them is still unknown. The Nazis may have praised Wagner's operas, but one has only to try to imagine the iconoclastic Siegfried in a totalitarian society like Nazi Germany to realize the essential antithesis between such a society and the heathen spirit.

Out of the Shadows

When a great tree is destroyed, it may appear extinct, but if the tree is strong, from its roots new shoots may still grow. The first heathen rebirth in Germany was a blighted growth. In the revulsion of feeling against all things heathen that followed World War II, it might have seemed that another thousand years must pass before the tree could sprout anew. Certainly, it will be some time before symbols like the swastika can be publicly displayed (which is a pity, since the swastika is a sun symbol used to invoke luck and prosperity in native folk art from Asia to North America), but the religion itself transcends its symbols, and the time for its rebirth had come.

Oddly enough, the English-speaking world was reawakened to the call of the North by the work of the very Christian J.R.R.Tolkien. Tolkien was a committed Roman Catholic, but he was also a professor of philology whose specialty was Germanic languages, and that Germanic awareness infused the legend he created to delight the world. It was in *The Hobbit* and *The Lord of the Rings,* for instance, that many people first encountered the runes. Tolkien mined Norse mythology for names such as Gandalf ("Wand-Elf"), beings such as dwarves, elves, trolls, and orcs, the Anglo-Saxon culture of the Rohirrim, and plot elements like the theft of a cup from a dragon. There is, of course, a great deal in Tolkien's work that is original or drawn from other sources, but it is the story of "Middle Earth," and through that story the lure of "northerness" flowed to enchant the world.

Tolkien, of course, was not the only author to seek inspiration in Germanic mythology. C. S. Lewis fell in love with it as a young man and included a number of Norse elements in his Narnia books, although they are often found in the camp of the villains. In the 1930s, Robert E. Howard introduced Conan of Cimmeria and a land of hardy warriors, all of whom were inspired by his concept of the Germanic hero. My own introduction to the world of Norse myth came from the work of Poul Anderson, a Danish American science fiction writer whose first novel, *The Broken Sword,* I read at the Santa Monica public library when I was supposed to be doing my homework. Anderson was a prolific author who handled hard science fiction and fantasy equally well and had a unique gift for incorporating the flavor of the sagas into modern fiction. His Norse fantasies, such as *Hrolf Kraki's Saga, The Merman's Children, The Last Viking, The War of the Gods,* and *Mother of Kings,* are all well worth reading.

The Lord of the Rings became a worldwide best seller in the 1960s, that period of social and artistic ferment during which the world awakened to the possibility of change. One of the things that was changing was the realization that we needed some of the things that the march of history had left behind and that they not only should, but could be restored. Renaissance Faires and historical re-creation groups such as the Society for Creative Anachronism sprang up. At the same time, groups in many countries were exploring the pre-Christian religions of their own lands.

Else Christensen founded the Odinist Fellowship in 1969 in Florida, and in 1971 Stephen McNallen started the Viking Brotherhood, which in 1976 became the Ásatrú Free Assembly (AFA). In Australia, the Odinic religion founded by A. Rud Mills was suppressed during World War II and revived in 1972. The Odinic Rite was founded in 1973 by John Yeowell in England. Even more significant were the efforts of the Icelandic poet and farmer Sveinbjorn Beinteinsson to gain acceptance for Ásatrú in his country. In 1973, the Icelandic Parliament voted to recognize the religion and give it the same state support accorded other faiths. These first heathen groups focused on Scandinavian heathenism, but in 1976 Garman Lord founded the Theodish tradition, which draws its inspiration from the heathen Anglo-Saxons. This eventually became the inspiration for a constellation of groups focusing on various Germanic tribal traditions.

During the 1980s, as might be expected, the existing groups evolved and additional organizations were founded or took their place. In 1986, the Ásatrú Free Assembly dissolved and in 1988 its assets were donated to the Ásatrú Alliance founded by Valgard Murray. In 1987, Edred Thorsson and James Chisholm founded the Troth (sometimes called the Ring of Troth) in Texas. Both organizations also started magazines, the Troth's *Idunna* and the Ásatrú Alliance's *Vor Tru.* Though known primarily as a Druid organization, the ADF (Ar n'Draoight Fein) also includes Heathen groves. This decade also saw the birth of numerous local kindreds.

The 1990s were a period of expansion and development, during which heathen organizations grew and developed their own philosophies and practices. In 1994, McNallen refounded the AFA as the Ásatrú Folk Assembly, with an increasing emphasis on White ethnicity. The Troth, on the other hand, became an international organization that was explicitly inclusive, welcoming people of all ethnicities and gender identities. Books on heathenism began to appear from commercial publishers, including Thorsson's books on rune lore and Kveldulf Gundarsson's *Teutonic Magic* and *Teutonic Religion*. The runes were also covered by Freya Aswynn in *Northern Mysteries and Magic*. Individuals and organizations published more specialized works, including the first edition of *Our Troth* by the Troth.

The first two decades of the twenty-first century have seen a steady growth of interest in Heathenry, with more organizations and publications in both the U.S. and Europe in print and online, including my own *Taking Up the Runes*, and the vastly expanded two-volume edition of *Our Troth* in 2006. Popular culture has also discovered heathen themes. Neil Gaiman's 2001 publication of *American Gods*, led to a popular TV series in 2017. The Marvel Universe movies made Thor and Loki popular heroes, and starting in 2013 the Vikings TV series served up a digest of northern history. Norse-themed musical groups like Wardruna and Heilung draw standing-room only crowds.

Unfortunately, in recent years the polarization afflicting the larger culture has led to an increasing division between inclusive Heathen organizations like the Troth and those that restrict membership on racial lines such as the Ásatrú Folk Assembly, as reported in recent studies by Snook (2015), Schnurbein (2016), and Calico (2018). Greater visibility also makes heathen symbols vulnerable to misuse by extremists, but websites and e-lists strengthen the bonds between those heathens who stand against them.

The seeds already planted are firmly rooted, and as we shall see in the chapters that follow, no matter what winds may blow, in the twenty-first century the heathen tree is reaching for the skies.

ROUND TWO

Gods and Goddesses

CHAPTER 6

The Gods

The first round has been completed. Karen brings the horn back to Janet as Thorolf picks up a bottle of mead. This also has been home brewed. After the first bottle was opened five years ago, the kindred swore to put the rest of the batch aside to mature, and with great self-control have kept from tasting it until now. This is a tense moment, since there is always the possibility that the brew has turned to vinegar instead. Thorolf gets the cork out, pours a little into a glass, and tastes. As they watch, he begins to smile.

"Oh yes..." he sighs. "This one is truly worthy of the gods." He turns to Janet and pours the mead into the horn. "I dedicate this mead to the Aesir and the Vanir. Their gifts to us have been great, and a gift demands a gift again!" He draws the rune Gebo over the horn.

Janet turns the horn so that its point is down and a little to the side and lifts it. "I drink to Thor, our protector and friend. I want to thank you for sending that tornado across the fields instead of through our town. Keep your hammer between us and the jotnar who would destroy, and teach us how to honor the helpful ones, especially Earth, your mother." Carefully, she drinks, then hands the horn to Karen to begin the circuit of the room.

Ásatrú is the troth of the gods, and it is the gods and goddesses who are the focus of the religion as it is practiced today. The principal male deities listed by Snorri in the *Younger Edda* (in Old Norse spelling) are Odhinn, Thórr, Baldr, Njordh and his son Freyr, Tyr, Bragi, Heimdallr, Hodr, Vidar, Vali, Ullr, and Forseti. Another figure who plays an important part in the mythology is Loki. One can also group the Germanic deities by family. The Vanir, who came to Asgard in an exchange of hostages after a war with the Aesir, consist of Njordh and his children Frey and Freyja. We know Nerthus only from a first-century Roman account, but today she is counted among the Vanir as well. The Aesir include all the other male deities, and Frigg, her handmaidens, and probably Idunn. Skadhi, Gerd, Hella, and possibly Sif come from the jotun kin. Nobody really knows about Loki, though it has been suggested that his father was a giant and his mother one of the Aesir.

To completely cover all the gods and goddesses would make up a hefty volume all by itself. In this and the next chapter, I will only be able to cover the deities who seem to be most active in the heathen world today. God names are given in the most common Anglicized spellings. For a more exhaustive presentation, I recommend the first volume of *Our Troth*. You will also find more information and some fine invocations in Galina Krasskova's *Exploring the Northern Tradition*. For a discussion of heathen rituals, see chapter 8. For more poetry in honor of the gods, try *Idunna* 63 (Spring 2005), which is available as a back issue from the Troth (see the resources section and bibliography for more information). Music for the songs for each deity can be found on my Web site, www.hrafnar.org.

Heimdall

The way to Asgard lies across Bifrost Bridge, the shimmering rainbow that spans the skies. It ends at a hall called Himinbjorg, where the god Heimdall watches with eyes that can see a hundred leagues and listens with ears that can hear the grass growing, needing no sleep in his ceaseless vigil as warder of the gods. He is called the white god, and most people visualize him as being tall and fair. He has a horse called Gulltopp (Golden-Top).

Of all the gods, Heimdall is the one who is most consistently benevolent to humankind. Perhaps this is because in the days before he became the gods' watchman he visited Midgard and fathered children there. Thus, "Heimdall's kin" include not only the gods, but humans. In the *Poetic Edda,* we are told that under the name of Ríg, he spent one night each with "great-grandfather" and "great-grandmother," "grandfather" and "grandmother," and "father" and "mother," and nine months later, each wife gave birth to a son. The child of the oldest couple became the ancestor of all thralls, the next was the father of free farmers, and by "mother" he sired the noble class. The youngest son of "Earl" became a runemaster and king, leading some to suspect that Ríg may be Odin rather than Heimdall.

According to Snorri, Heimdall himself is the son of Odin by the nine waves of the sea. One of his bynames, Vindhlér, means either "Wind-Sea" or "Wind-Protection." In folklore, the waves are called sheep, and the last wave in a sequence is the ram. The Old Norse word for *ram* is *heimdali,* so the sheep is considered one of his animals. Another of his bynames, Hallinskidhi, is a poetic word for a ram. Another creature with whom he is associated is the seal, whose form he took to fight Loki, who had stolen Freyja's necklace. He guards the forces of life, and at the end of the age he will summon the gods to battle by blowing the Gjallr horn.

As a god who guards the boundary of Asgard, and an ancestor of humankind, we can call on Heimdall for aid in warding ourselves and our homes. As ancestor of different human groups, he has an interest in helping people to get along. For this reason, the rune I use to represent him is Mannaz, ᛗ. Although he will play his part at Ragnarök (he and Loki will slay each other), and he owns a sword, he is generally peaceful in character.

If you live on a seacoast, one way to get close to Heimdall is to sit on the shore and watch the waves rolling in. Visualize the god rising from the frothing surf, shining as the sun gleams on the sea. You may also seek him on mountain tops or bridges. Read the "Lay of Ríg" in the *Elder Edda*, meditate on the tasks performed by each of Ríg's offspring, and identify their equivalents in your own life. Praise him whenever you see a rainbow. The Viking Symposium that I attended in 2000 opened in St. John's, Newfoundland, the easternmost harbor of North America and gateway to the New World. As I went walking on the heights above the town, I saw a rainbow arching overhead and felt Heimdall very near.

A *blót*, or blessing, is usually performed for a specific deity. To honor Heimdall, dress the altar in white and gold. You may add pictures of waves, sheep, seals, and so on. Fill the drinking horn with mead or Ramshead beer. For the feast, you may cook seafood or lamb. No day of the week is directly associated with Heimdall, but as guardian of the gate, he can be honored at the beginning of the week, on Monday.

The following is an invocation to Heimdall:

> Holy Heimdall, hear thy children,
> Warden, open wide the way,
> Bifrost blazes now before us,
> The Road of Ríg we ride today.
> Friend and father, grant us favor
> As all things thou dost see and hear.
> Choose for thy children sight unclouded,
> Speech and understanding clear.

You may also sing the following chant:

> Heimdall, Heimdall, wisest of watchers,
> Bifrost Bridge now blazes bright.
> Open wide the way of welcome,
> The Aesir fare to feast tonight.

Tyr

Tyr is the god who gives his name to Tuesday. The Romans identified him with Mars, their god of war, but Tyr is much more. His name is derived from the same Indo-European root that gave us the Greek *Zeus*, so he must originally have been a sky god. He is one of the two gods for whom a rune is named: Tiwaz (Anglo-Saxon Tir), ↑. This element may surivive in the Anglo-Saxon Rune Poem, "Tir is a guiding star, keeps faith well with princes; it is on course over night's mists, never failing." His most ancient holy places were on mountain tops, close to the sky.

But an early Germano-Roman dedication to "Mars Thingsus" (Mars of the Assembly) suggests that he was also seen as a god of sovereignty and right order, and this aspect survived in the lore. In the Viking Age, Tyr was invoked for victory in battle, but it seems likely that it was not war that concerned him, but the *holmgang*—the trial by combat that was the final court of appeal.

By the Viking Age, although Tyr was known to be both wise and brave, only two stories about him survived. In the "Lay of Hymir," he and Thor go to Jotunheim to seek a cauldron big enough to brew beer for all the gods. His role here is minor, and the poem is important chiefly because it indicates that Tyr comes from giant kin.

The second and only tale in which Tyr plays a major role is the story of the binding of the wolf Fenris, told in the *Prose Edda*. The wolf was one of Loki's children by the giantess Angrboda. For a time, the gods kept him in Asgard, and Tyr was the only one with the courage to feed him. But the wolf kept growing and eating, until it became clear that if he were not contained he would destroy them all. The gods attempted to bind Fenris, but he broke every fetter they could create until they got the dwarves to craft the fetter called Gleipnir, which was made from six impossible things: the sound of a cat's footfall, a woman's beard, the mountain's roots, a bear's sinews, a fish's breath, and bird's spittle. When it was done, they called the wolf to try it on him, promising he could break it easily, but this time Fenris suspected a trick and refused to be bound unless one of the gods would set his hand in the wolf's mouth as insurance.

The only one who dared to do so was Tyr, and when the fetter proved unbreakable, Fenris bit off his hand. Here we see the paradox of the god whose essence is integrity participating in a deception. As a result, the god who aids the warrior has no sword hand. The god who raised the wolf is the one who binds him. Violence controls violence. Following this example of sacrifice, we find the courage to bind the wolves within our own souls.

We have no descriptions of Tyr's appearance. I usually visualize him as being rather lean, with grizzled dark hair and gray eyes and a somewhat grim or thoughtful expression, wearing a mail shirt and a cloak of dark red wool. Today, although some follow Tyr as a disciplined warrior, others honor him as an example of integrity and self-sacrifice for the common good—he was, after all, the only one of the gods willing to pay the price for deceiving the wolf. He is therefore seen as a god of justice, and those who call on him for help in that area had better be certain they are in the right, because true justice is what they will receive. We call on him for help in understanding and making the hard choices and fulfilling the oaths we have sworn. He is often sought by those involved in law, law enforcement, and the military.

To know Tyr, we must be willing to see ourselves clearly, to recognize our faults and do our best to correct them, and to deal honorably with others. The best gift we can offer him is to fulfill our obligations to the earth, to the community, and to the gods. But if you want to honor him in ritual, for instance, to ask his help in a legal case or his protection for kinfolk serving in wartime, you might cover the altar in a dark red cloth and fill the horn with a robust red wine such as Bull's Blood. Food for the feast might include roast beef and rough dark bread.

Tyr's symbols include the severed hand or glove, the star, and the Irminsul, a column that the tenth-century chronicler Widukind tells

us was set up by the Saxons in honor of Mars to celebrate a victory
and cut down by Charlemagne. The Irminsul is a world axis, linking
heaven and earth.

The following is an invocation:

> Tyr, hear our summons! Undefeated defender
> And lord of the Allthing, lend us aid now!
> As Fenris you fed, of the Beast you were binder,
> One hand—winning renown—bless now our battle!
> Be now our star, bright beacon in darkness,
> Secure as the Irminsul, now may we stand.
> Lord of justice, receive this offering!

Or sing:

> Tyr, we praise thee on this day,
> Protection grant from those who slay;
> Fetter fear, the victory win,
> Bind the wolves without, within!

Odin

In the *Younger Edda*, when Gylfi asks "Who is the highest and
most ancient of all the gods," the High One gives twelve names, beginning with All-father. Later, he identifies this powerful figure as
Odin. Given that the speaker of "Havamál" (the words of the High
One) is also identified with Odin, the being who is telling all this to
Gylfi is clearly Odin himself. We should not be surprised that the
god who is most associated with words and language should have
more names than any other. Neil Price (2002) lists 188 bynames
from Old Norse literature. And then, of course, there are the Anglo-

Saxon and Continental German versions of his name: Woden, Wotan, and Wodanaz.

The categories into which these names may be grouped tell us a great deal about the god. Since the poets made their living praising kings, it is only to be expected that many of the names for the god who was (among other things) patron of both kings and skalds have to do with war and aggression, frenzy and anger. However, there are many others that relate to wisdom, divinity, and magic. Other names refer to Odin's power over the dead. There are names that describe Odin as a trickster and master of disguise, and others that call him a giver of pleasure and prosperity. Some speak of him as a wanderer or a weather god. Descriptive names tell us that he has a long, hoary beard and a drooping moustache, is lean, has a straight forehead, and wears a shaggy cloak and a floppy hat. Although occasionally he appears as a younger man, most heathens see him as gray bearded but vigorous, with an eye patch covering his missing eye.

The rune most associated with Odin is Ansuz, or Ás, ᚠ, meaning a god. The Anglo-Saxon version is Oss, "a mouth." However, the root of the god's primary name, *Odh*, means "frenzy"—not in the sense of madness so much as the kind of ecstasy in which one learns, understands, and creates. In the myth of human creation, Odin and his brothers found a log of ashwood and one of elm and made them into the first man and the first woman. The gift of Odin was breath, the catalyst that activates body and spirit and makes us live. Many find that the god comes closest in the wind that whispers in the trees, the wind that is the breath of the world.

Although Odin is called All-father and plays a central role in the life of Asgard, rather than being the "king" of the gods, he acts more like the chairman of the board. When decisions must be made, the gods gather in council. The rest of the time, Odin wanders the worlds. His purpose in so doing is to learn, and what he learns he brings back and shares. Among his gifts are the mead of poetry, which he won from the giantess Gunnlodh; the runes, which he gained through the sacrifice of self to self, hanging for nine days and nights on the World Tree; and wisdom, for which he traded one of his eyes at Mimir's Well. Which eye it was is debated, but some believe that while the eye in his head sees the outer world, he is always viewing the inner dimensions with the eye that is in the Well.

When the other gods receded from human awareness, Odin continued to wander, at least he is the Norse deity we find most often appearing in modern literature. His struggles to reconcile the claims of love, freedom, and power are at the center of Richard Wagner's *Ring* operas. More recently, he has appeared as "The Raven" in Michael Scott Rohan's *Winter of the World* trilogy, as "Mr. Wednesday" in Neil Gaiman's *American Gods,* and we strongly suspect him of being the "Raven King" in Susannah Clarke's *Jonathan Strange and Mr. Norrell.*

These days, Odin is sought by (or seeks out) those who work with words and people involved in the creative arts generally; those who study magic, especially the runes; and students, scholars, scientists, and others who seek knowledge. He can be considered a god of evolving consciousness. However I advise against calling on him if all you want is victory and glory. Odin is very much concerned with the future of the world. He will take those who dedicate themselves to him and use them, as he sacrificed himself, for the greater good. Those who encounter him find him a very powerful personality, who sometimes rather unexpectedly inserts himself into people's lives. Butting heads with Odin can be painful, and perhaps for this reason, women, or those who are spiritually receptive, may have a more productive relationship with him than macho men. *Othroerir,* by Laure Lynch (2005) tells the story of one woman's experiences with Odin.

We are connected to Odin by every breath we take and every word we speak, but if you want to show him especial honor, the ideal time to do so is on Wednesday—"Wodan's Day." Colors generally associated with him are the deep blue of the moonlit sky at midnight, black, and silver or gray, as are the numbers 3 and 9. His creatures are the ravens Hugin and Munin, who bring him news of all the worlds, and his wolves Geri and Freki. He rides the eight-legged horse Sleipnir. Odin's hall is Valhall, in the part of Asgard called Gladsheim, but he visits his wife, Frigg, at Fensalir. Favored offerings include mead, akvavit, smoked salmon, and rare beef. The *valknut* on the cover of this book is his symbol.

To honor Odin, it is best to write your own poetry, but the following is something with which to begin:

> High One, Just as High and Third
> These are his names as we have heard,
> Wide of Wisdom counsel gives,
> Odin, Oski, Omi lives,
> We call on Wodan, Vili, Ve,
> to All-father, Sigfather, Gandfather pray.
>
> Odin, Oski, Joy ordaining,
> Wotan, wish lord, well beloved
> To thy delight let us drink deeply—
> All-father, to our feast be welcome!

And a song:

> Wild, on the wind you ride,
> Wise, in the heart abide,
> Wanderer, at my side,
> Wodan draw near.

Thor

A survey of the sagas will leave you with the impression that half the inhabitants of Iceland had names beginning with "Thor" or "Tor." Place names from Germany to Iceland bear witness to the popularity of the god. The Romans identified him with their own thunder god, Jupiter, and his day, Thursday, was a market day and holiday. Where Odin was considered the patron of kings and of the skalds who praised them, it was Thor Thunderer who ruled the weather on which farmers and fishermen depended and who was the great defender against physical and spiritual dangers.

Unlike Odin, Thor is only dangerous to his enemies. In the "Lay of Hárbard": 23, Thor tells us that he has been killing giants in the east. But this is not simply destruction for the fun of it. "Much might had the etins if all did live. Little might had men in Midgard's round." In other words, as Champion of Asgard, Thor's job is to keep the balance between human beings and the elder powers. Not all etins are evil—Thor's father was Odin, but his mother was the giantess Jordh (Earth), and he has two sons, Modhi and Magni, by another giantess, Jarnsaxa.

In the *Eddas*, Thor is presented as a mighty warrior with a red beard, whose laughter rumbles like the thunder he rules. The rune most often used to represent him is Thurisaz, ᚦ, whose sound begins his name. He drives a cart drawn by two goats, Tanngniostr and Tanngrisnir, and he is armed with his famous hammer, Mjolnir, which his belt of strength and iron gloves enable him to wield. His lands are at Thruthvangar and his hall is called Bilskirnir, in which there are 540 sleeping places. The lady of that hall is his wife, Sif, by whom he has a daughter called Thruth (or Trude), which means "strength."

Some of the best stories in Norse mythology are about Thor. In the "Lay of Hymir," he challenges the giants in feats of strength. In the "Lay of Thrym," he has to go to Jotunheim disguised as a bride to reclaim his hammer. However, in the "Lay of Alvis" he uses his wits to win a riddle game with a dwarf who is trying to claim his daughter. When Thor fights, it is as a single champion, but on his journeys his companion is often Loki—they are the original "odd couple." When Loki insults the gods at a drinking party ("The Flyting of Loki"), Thor is the only one who can kick him out of the hall.

Thor is one of the most popular of the gods today. His hammer remains the symbol of heathen faith. We call on him for protection, courage, and the energy to face our own challenges, physical or spiritual. And when the jotnar are out of balance and a wildfire or a superstorm approaches, we call on him to protect our homes.

At a feast, Thor is honored with a hearty beer such as Stout or Bock (or in Canada, Iron Hammer beer) and plenty of food. Most appropriate is a haunch of goat, but be careful not to break the bones, as Thor has the power to restore his steeds to life if an emergency forces him to eat them ("Gylfaginning": 44), but a broken bone will make the goat go lame. If goat is not available, a good roast of beef will do. Most consider bright red to be his color.

The following is the invocation I use for Thor. Of course, I live in California, where rain is often needed. Elsewhere, you might ask him to bring sunshine.

> Redbeard, firebeard, bringer of lightning,
> Life-giving stormlord, lover of feasting,
> Father of freedom, fighter most doughty,
> Donar, defender, dearly we need thee,
> Hear us now, hero, hasten to help us,
> Gifts thy great goats gallop to bring.
> Prosper thy people: pour on earth plenty,
> Rain in abundance, right for the season.

And a song:

> Thor bashes etins, Thor trashes trolls!
> When he swings his hammer, oh how the thunder rolls—
> With a clash and a clatter,
> Our foes he has scattered
> From Midgard!

Freyr

Second only to Thor in popularity during the Viking Age was Freyr, whose name means "Lord." He was the god to whom folk prayed for peace and, as giver of rain and sunshine, good seasons. Freyr is one of the Vanir, gods of a different clan (possibly originally the gods of a different Germanic group) who fought "the first war in the world" with the Aesir. The conflict ended in a draw and was resolved with an exchange of hostages. One of the Vanic deities who came to live in Asgard was Freyr.

The Vanir are often dismissed as "fertility deities," and the amulets showing Freyr with an erect phallus certainly indicate that he is a god of masculine potency. But he is also called Yngvi or Ing, ancestor of the early Swedish kings. Although the sea kings of the Viking Age sacrificed to Odin for victory in battle, Freyr is the god of sovereignty.

Of course, sovereignty, in the old days, was inextricably linked to fertility. The vigor of the king ensured the vitality of the land. In Snorri Sturlusson's history of the Norse kings and Saxo Grammaticus's history of the Danes, we hear of rulers who were sacrificed to renew the land and of successful kings who received offerings after death so that they might continue to bless it.

The seed shape of the rune Ingwaz ($\diamond$) tells us that Freyr is the god of the grain in all its phases—vigorously erect in the springtime, cut down at harvest, and buried in the ground so that it may sprout once more. All virile male animals, both wild and tame, may be considered his, but he is particularly associated with the boar (a golden boar, Gullinbursti, is his steed), the stallion (the one he rides is Blodughofi—"Bloody-hooves"), and because the weapon he will use at Ragnarök is an antler, with the stag.

Today, Freyr is invoked for potency and prosperity. Straight men see him as a model and women as a lover. In Viking times, some considered his worship effeminate because in Uppsala he was served by priests who danced for him with an "unmanly clatter" of bells, so many gay men find in him a patron as well. It should be noted that in the Viking period, "unmanliness" consisted of taking the submissive role in sex, not in being attracted to men. For a discussion of this question, see my article "Sex, Status, and Seidh: Homosexuality in Germanic Religion" (www.seidh.org/articles/sex-status-seidh.html).

Despite his virility, Freyr is known to have had only one romance. In the "Lay of Skirnir," we are told how, seeing the jotun maid Gerd from afar, he falls deeply in love and sends his servant, Skirnir, to arrange the marriage. Persuading the maiden takes both threats and magic, but eventually she agrees to meet with Freyr nine nights later in the grove of Barri. It has been suggested that her name refers to the walled garth within which crops can be safely grown and that their union refers in some way to the taming of the wilderness. So far as we know, once they are married, Freyr remains faithful.

Today, Freyr is one of the most popular deities. I see him as young and handsome, with wheat-gold hair. One feels his presence in field and forest and wherever productive work is being done. We ask him for prosperity and fertility of mind or body. He enjoys celebrations of all kinds. When my kindred honors Freyr, the focus of the feast is usually the biggest pork roast we can find, accompanied by barley and whatever else people want to make that's rich and yummy. A Freyrsman cooked the best barbecue I ever had.

Colors associated with Freyr are green and dark brown or black. A Freyr altar is often decorated with antlers, greenery, and heads of grain. Some Freyr priests wear a belt sewn with bells. I invoke the god with the following poem:

> Hail, lord Freyr! All hail to the great god,
> Helper of humankind, hail!
> Father of the fertile field, fairest of fighters,
> Bestow thy blessings now.
> Thou art the offspring of Njorth and of Nerthus,

In Alfheim all adore thee.
Thy glory has melted the heart of the maiden—
We hail thee, husband of Gerd!
Frodi the fruitful, fill now our meadows
with crowds of calves and cows;
Sceaf of the Scyldings, soon let us gather
gladly your golden grain;
As Ingvi we will hail thee, ever returning,
In thy wagon we worship thee still.
The bright boar, Gullinbursti, bears thee to bless us,
Sun-bright splendor of life—
Strong as a stallion, thy phallus fulfills us,
Lord and lover, let us live anew!

And a song:

Cattle in pasture and grain in the field,
From all of our workings a bountiful yield,
Peace and fulfillment, pleasure and power,
Freyr, join our feasting, for this is your hour!

Njordh

The father of Freyr was also one of the Vanic hostages. Like his son, Njordh is a god of prosperity, but his field of endeavor is the sea. His hall is Nóatún, which means "shipyard." In the *Younger Edda* ("Gylfaginning": 23), we are told that he rules wind, sea, and fire and governs the success of sea voyages and fishing. Even more than his children he is a god of wealth, who can "grant wealth of land or possessions to those who pray to him for this."

It is said that among the Vanir, brother and sister could marry, and for this reason some believe that the goddess Nerthus was Njordh's original wife and mother of Freyr and Freyja. This idea is based on the similarity of name and (as we shall see in the next chapter) function. However, since our only knowledge of Nerthus comes from a first-century Roman writer, and our information on Njordh from the Viking Age, it must remain a theory. In Norse myth, we are told that after Njordh had moved to Asgard he eventually married the jotun maid Skadhi, who was required to choose her husband from among the gods by looking at their feet. Those of Njordh were the most beautiful (and probably, since he was often in the water, the cleanest), and so he became her husband. However, the marriage did not prosper. When they stayed at her house, he was kept awake by the howling of the wolves, and when they stayed at his, the seagulls woke her far too early, so they agreed to live separately, though apparently they remained good friends.

I picture Njordh as a robust man of middle years, with dark hair beginning to go gray. He is barefoot, wearing a sailor's short breeches and a sleeveless tunic, and probably some gold jewelry as well. In my opinion, the ideal place to honor Njordh would be at a beach party, complete with barbecue, volleyball, and lots of frothy beer. We offer him beers with nautical names or champagne. Salmon and other fish go on the barbecue. His symbols include the ship and the outline of a bare foot. His colors are sea green and gold.

The following is an invocation for Njordh:

> Fair-footed father of Freyr and Freyja,
> Wave-rider, winning us wealth from the sea,
> Shielder of ships, send us good fortune,
> Hear us and help us to prosperous harbor,
> Bring us a blessing, oh brother of Nerthus,
> Pledge of the Vanir, by our prayers be pleased
> In Nóatún, oh Njordh, know now our need.

And a chant:

> Over the sea a shining ship comes sailing,
> The Giving God has gained the golden shore.
> Abundance he brings for every need availing,
> Steer our ships safely in, goodfather Njordh!

Loki

Steer clear of Loki if you have problems with ambiguity. However you relate to reality, you should deal with him carefully. Loki plays a major role in the tales of the gods. Some believe that he is the offspring of a goddess and a giant—certainly, he often seems to play the role of intermediary between them. Like Coyote in Native American myth, Loki is a troublemaker and a culture-bringer, the latter often as a result of the former.

Although the name *Loki* is not in fact related to "Löge," the similarity led Richard Wagner to identify Loki with the element of fire in the *Ring* operas, and the association has stuck. People often picture him as lithe and active, with fox-red hair. Like fire, he can be a good servant or a dangerous enemy.

In the stories, Loki often causes trouble, but in making reparation, he brings benefits. For instance, after cutting off the hair of the goddess Sif, he gets the dwarves to compete in making marvelous gifts for the gods that include not only replacement hair but also Freyr's magic ship, Odin's spear, and Thor's hammer. To keep the giant from taking Freyja, the sun, and the moon as his fee for building the walls of Asgard, Loki turns himself into a mare in season to distract the giant's stallion. Nine months later, the mare gives birth to the eight-legged horse Sleipnir, who becomes Odin's steed.

But the horse is not Loki's only offspring. By the giantess Angr-bodha, he is the father of the Midgard serpent, Hella, and the wolf Fenris (who later bit off Tyr's hand). For a long time, he was an accepted, if not popular, part of the Asgard community, but after his involvement in the killing of Odin's son, Baldr, the gods turned against him, and eventually he was captured and bound in Hel beneath a serpent that drips venom. His wife, Sigyn, holds a bowl to catch it, but when she has to empty the bowl the venom strikes his face and his struggles cause earthquakes.

If you want to start a "spirited" discussion among heathens, ask whether Loki should be honored in ritual. Some, in particular those who follow the Theodish traditions, abhor him to the point where they will not allow his name to be mentioned in the hall. Others point out that he brings gifts as well as troubles and will hold a blót for him with cinnamon schnaps or peppered vodka in which you toss a dram into the fire each time you drink to him. However, you should bear in mind that Loki is a trickster, and unless you are experienced in dealing with chaotic forces, it might be better not to attract his attention.

We are told in "The Flyting of Loki" that Odin once swore that whenever he got a drink Loki should have one too, so in our kindred, we compromise by pouring out a bit for Loki whenever the horn is passed for Odin. Although he can be seen as a devil figure, Loki is also sometimes cited as a trickster and iconoclast who fulfills the necessary function of upsetting preconceptions and shaking up false certainties.

If you do decide to honor Loki, put some humor in it:

> There once was a being called Loki
> And though some of his dealings were hokey,
> When he got in a tangle,
> Some solution he'd wangle,
> And make everything okey-dokey.

Or you might sing the following verse from the pagan version of "Gimme That Ol' Time Religion":

> Let us all go worship Loki.
> He's the Nordic god of chaos,
> Which is why this verse does not rhyme or sync
> Or scan or nuthin'.

Note: This table is based on information in the lore, along with some personal inspiration, and should not be considered authoritative.

Deity	Day	Rune	Color(s)	Food	Totems	Tools	Place
HEIMDALL	Monday?	ᛉ	white	Ramshead, beer, mead	ram, seal	horn, sword	Himinbjorg
TYR	Tuesday	↑	dark red, sky blue	red wine, beef	dog	sword	Irminsul
ODIN	Wednesday	ᚠ	blue, black, gray	mead, wine, akvavit, beef, salmon	raven, eagle, wolf, horse	spear	Gladsheim, Valhall, Hlithskjalf
THOR	Thursday	ᛉ	red, blue	Guinness, bock, goat	goat, eagle	hammer, oath ring	Thrutheim
FREYR	Friday	◇	green, brown	wheat, beer, pork, venison	boar, horse	antler	Alfheim

NJORDH	Saturday?	ᛚ	sea green	champagne, seafood	fish	boat	Nóatún
BALDR	Sunday?	ᚷ	gold	ale	daisy, mistletoe	Draupnir	Breithablik, Hel
IDUNN	Monday?	ᚦ	red, gold, light green	cider apples	apple trees	basket	orchard
SKADHI	Tuesday?	ᛁ	white, dark brown	vodka, wild game	wolves	spear	Thrymheim
FRIGG	Friday or Wednesday	ᛒ	white, pale blue	plum wine, birch beer, lamb	sheep, osprey, birch	spindle	Fensalir
SIF	Thursday	ᚾ	gold	wheat, beer, bread	wheat	comb	Thrutheim wheatfield
FREYJA	Friday	ᚠ	green, dark red	fruit, beer, pork	cats, sow, horse, falcon	necklace	Sessrumnir, Folkvangar
NERTHUS	Saturday?	ᛖ	brown	stout, vegetables	cow	ship	Midgard
HELLA	Sunday?	ᚺ	black/white	dark beer	horse	necklace	Hel

CHAPTER 7

The Goddesses

Karen brings the horn to Dave, who is called Ironhand because he is a blacksmith who has forged everything from the wrought-iron horn stand to the hand-crafted blades worn by some in the room. There are a few whispers as he smiles at the dark-haired girl beside him. This is the first time Dave has brought a guest to the hall.

"Tonight, I want to honor Frigg. A year ago I made an offering to her, asking her to find me a woman to share my life. This is Sofia. I met her at the Pagan Pride Parade last May, and she's agreed to marry me!" Now he's grinning from ear to ear.

"Hail Sofia!" "Hail Ironhand!" "Hail Frigg!" The hall erupts in cheering.

Freydis wonders why he didn't choose a heathen girl, but although in recent years many women have turned to the Germanic gods, there are still more unattached heathen men than heathen women.

"Freyr had to go to Jotunheim to find a bride," answers her husband, "and a lot of our guys have to go to the Wiccans. Sofia seems to be coping pretty well so far, but I bet she could use a friend. Why don't you take her under your wing?"

When the High One has told Gylfi who the gods are, in the *Younger Edda*, Just-as-High adds, "No less holy are the ásynjur [the goddesses], nor is their power less." Of the ásynjur, the highest is Frigg, followed by her handmaidens. Equally important is Freyja. Other goddesses with important roles in the mythology include Idunn, Sif, Skadhi, Gerd, and Hella. Today, many honor the continental goddesses Nerthus and Holda as well. As with the gods, to properly present all the goddesses would take another volume, so I must focus on those goddesses who are currently most active. For further information, I recommend the first volume of *Our Troth,* Galina Krasskova's *Exploring the Northern Tradition,* and my own articles on the goddesses, originally published in *Sagewoman* magazine and now available on my Web site at www.hrafnar.org/articles.html. The Web site also has music for the goddess songs.

Idunn

In scene two of Richard Wagner's opera *Das Rhinegold,* the gods fade and grow old because the giants have taken the goddess of the golden apples away. Although in the opera he confuses Idunn (Anglicized as Idunna) with Freyja, Wagner shows clearly the importance of the goddess from whose hands the gods receive the fruit that keeps them ever young. Along with Freyja, Idunn is the goddess the giants most desire, and indeed, at one point she is betrayed by Loki, kidnapped by the jotun Thiazi, and rescued by Loki again, who carries her back to Asgard in the form of a hazelnut. When the giant Thiazi tries to get her back, he is killed. In Asgard, she is the wife of Bragi, the singer to the gods.

The meaning of Idunn's name is "the renewing one" or "the active one." A similar term, *idhiagroen* ("renewed-green") is used for the world that will emerge after Ragnarök. In a poem from the beginning of the tenth century ("Haustlöng"), the complex word play compares Idunn to water bubbling over rocks and a grain field and calls her the playmate of the gods (North 1997). She can be seen as a goddess of spring who is rescued from winter's clutches to revitalize the earth. She brings forth life from death and renews the world. For this reason, many heathens, particularly in the Troth, see her as patroness of the resurrection of the Northern Tradition.

I usually see Idunn as a slender young woman with fair hair. Her colors seem to be gold, light green, and a rosy apple red. In her orchard, the trees are in all stages of growth, from flower to fruit to fallow. In an Idunnablót, we fill the horn with apple cider and pass out apple slices.

The following is an invocation for her:

> Holy fruit, in Asgard's heart hid,
> Grows in Idunna's girded garth:
> In leafless trees life is renewed,
> Silver blossoms star bare branches,
> Golden the apples given to gods,
> Sweet the fruit with its secret seeds.
>
> In Midgard's mirk, men wake from madness:
> In fields a thousand years left fallow,
> Sleeping seeds at last are sprouting—
> Idunna, see the new day dawning,
> Bear to us thy branch of blessings,
> a tree of troth to bless the true.

And a song:

> In Idunna's garden apples grow,
> Always in fruit and in flower.

Time cannot touch those who their sweetness know,
Blessings and bliss fill her bower.
Lady, but one portion give,
Like the holy gods we'll live,
Protected in peace by your power.

Skadhi

In the *Younger Edda,* we are told how a giant maiden once appeared at the gates of Asgard, fully armed and angry. Her name was Skadhi and she was the daughter of the giant Thiazi. As compensation for the death of her father, she asked that the gods award her his hall, Thrymheim, give her a husband from among them, and make her laugh. The hall was not a problem, but the gods required that she choose her husband by looking at his feet alone. She assumed that the most beautiful pair would belong to Baldr, but the feet she chose belonged to the old ship master Njordh. Loki finally got her to laugh by tying one end of a rope to the horns of a nanny goat and the other to his balls and letting himself be jerked about—a prime example of Viking humor.

Skadhi's marriage to Njordh was not very successful, as he hates the mountains and she can't stand living by the sea. In Norwegian tradition, she later took up with Odin and had sons by him who became the ancestors of several lines of Norse kings. According to the *Younger Edda* ("Gylfaginning": 23), Skadhi lives in the mountains, where she travels on snowshoes or skies and hunts game. As a hunting goddess, she is sometimes linked with Ullr.

In "The Flyting of Loki," Skadhi tells him that he will get cold counsel from her holy shrines and groves. This, and surviving place names, indicate that she did receive worship during the Viking Age. It also shows that she has not forgiven Loki for his role in the death of her father, and indeed it is she who places the serpent where it will drip venom on his face.

Skadhi is strongly associated with winter, when the wolves howl. But the snow shelters the earth as well. Some honor her at the Charming of the Plow ceremony that marks the transition from winter to spring. In addition to the wolves, she may be seen as the predator/protector of all wild beasts. In the human world, Skadhi is a patroness not only for hunting but also for all sports and is especially dear to independent women and those who do jobs usually associated with men.

We honor her with the white of snow and the dark brown of earth, and offer her iced vodka and rare red beef or venison.

A prayer for Skadhi goes:

> Skadhi, shining snowshoe goddess,
> Ice-bright beauty,
> With winter's white the earth you ward.
> Wise bride of gods;
> Your wild wolves run through wind and weather,
> Holy huntress, help us,
> Summon storms as is right for the season!
> Skadhi, I summon thee!

And a song:

> When wolves howl upon the mountain heights,
> Swift, beneath the northern lights,
> Skadhi comes skimming o'er the snow.
> When it goes,
> Her sweet buds will swell the bough,
> Earth will open to the plough.

Frigg

When I first began to work with Odin, it became clear that I would have to get to know his wife as well. The Fricka we see in Richard Wagner's operas is a vastly distorted version, based more on late classical views of Hera than on anything in the northern lore. I have found Frigg (or the Anglicized form, Frigga) to be a fascinating, multiaspected figure, almost as complex as Odin himself.

She is called the daughter of Fjorgyn, which would make her a child of the earth giants. Of her it is said that "she knows all fates but says nothing" ("Flyting of Loki": 29). One has the sense that she is the still center to which Odin always returns from his wanderings. She is also, however, a giver of sovereignty, who in several stories arranges for lordship to be awarded to individuals or tribes. Her protection can be powerful, but she is unable to save Baldr, her son. Because of that loss, she has great sympathy for those who grieve.

Properly speaking, our name for Friday comes from Frigg's name, but this is based on an identification of Frigg with Venus, who is really more like Freyja than Frigg. Of course, it is possible that the two were originally a single figure, but they had become very different by the end of the Viking Age. Some heathens prefer to honor Freyja and Freyr on Friday and to work with Frigg on Wednesday along with her husband. The meaning of the rune Berkano (ᛒ) seems to fit Frigg's qualities, and thus the birch tree is associated with her as well. Her cart is drawn by rams, so she probably has a flock of sheep. For this reason, and because weaving was a major occupation for Norse women, we think of her as a patroness of spinning, weaving, and all fiber arts. She also upholds the Germanic tradition of good housekeeping, and those who work with her will find themselves motivated to do some cleaning.

The name of Frigg's home, Fensalir, means the hall in the marshes. We associate wading birds such as the blue heron with her as well. Like Freyja, she has a falcon cloak—probably that of the sea eagle or osprey. Many heathens have independently had the impression that her colors are white and pale blue. Because her cart is drawn by rams, lamb and mutton are offered to her at feasts. She can be honored with mead or plum wine.

In the *Younger Edda*, Snorri tells us that Frigg is attended by twelve handmaidens, some of whom appear in other references. They can be viewed as separate goddesses or as forms Frigg takes to work in the world. These demigoddesses are:

1. *Fulla, who guards the secret of the mysteries.* Snorri tells us that she is a virgin, with flowing hair held by a gold band. She carries the treasure casket of Frigg, looks after her footwear, and shares her secrets. Fulla seems to be a threshold figure who holds the visible symbol of the mysteries. Her tokens are the golden headband and the casket she bears.

2. *Sága, who knows all the old tales.* Sága has her own palace, Sökkvabek ("Sunken Hall"), where according to Snorri she drinks with Odin out of golden cups and they tell each other stories. Sága knows the names of the ancestors and all the family histories. She counsels the dísir and speaks through every old grandmother who preserves the box of family photos and remembers the old ways. Her tokens are a golden cup or a book of stories.

3. *Eir, the ancient healer.* Eir is said by Snorri to be "an extremely good physician." The name is also included among "Odin's maids," the rest of whom are elsewhere given as valkyries, but here described as norns who shape necessity. Eir is the healer of the gods. Even though her origins are mysterious, they are linked by her skills to the shaping of fate. We can assume that she practices the

kinds of medicine traditional to women, strongly based in the lore of herbs, food, and spells. She appears stern but compassionate. Her tokens are the mortar and pestle.

4. *Gefjun, who gives before we even know our need.* Gefjun is said by Snorri to be a virgin, who welcomes all who die unmarried. Her name means "giver" and is also an epithet of Freyja. She appears independently as a Danish goddess who is married to Scyld, and she is the mother of giants who in ox-form created Zealand by ploughing off a piece from the mainland. She had a sanctuary at Leire and a neck ring gained by making love with a young man. Gefjun can be seen as the path where Freyja and Frigg meet. But in Frigg's hall, Gefjun gives as a mother gives. Her token today is the basket or cornucopia.

5. *Sjöfn, the one who inclines the heart to love.* According to Snorri she directs the minds of men and women to love and gives her name to "affection" (*siafni*). Today, we feel that Sjöfn's power extends far beyond the simple attractions of lust or romantic love. She governs the whole web of affectional relationships by which women maintain family unity, including the love of siblings, parents, and children and the affection that grows between those who work together. A token for her is a rose-colored stone heart on a golden chain.

6. *Lofn, who gives us permission to follow our dreams.* Lofn's name is related to the Old Norse words for *permission* and *praise*. Snorri tells us that she is the one who asks Frigg and Odin to allow unions between those forbidden to love by

society. By extension, Lofn gives permission not only for love affairs but also for us to do all those things that our own mental blocks or society's opinion forbid, including developing or exercising our personal and spiritual power. Her token is a golden key.

7. *Syn, who guards our boundaries.* Syn guards the door of Frigg's hall and denies entry to those who are not supposed to enter. She is appointed as a defense in assemblies against matters that she wishes to refute. The word *Syn* means "a denial," saying "no."

Syn wards the physical doors that keep danger from entering our homes and the gates to our personal and psychic space. She gives us the strength to say "no." She can be invoked when warding a house or sacred space or to create a shield that can withstand personal or psychic attack. She appears at the door of Frigg's hall wearing gray and holding a staff. Her token is the birch broom hung over the door to banish evil.

8. *Hlín, who defends us.* Hlín is the one who protects those Frigg wants to save and the refuge of those who are in danger. She represents Frigg in the lines "Another woe awaiteth Hlin, when forth goes Odin to fight the Wolf" ("Voluspa": 52). Scholars generally agree that her first woe was the death of Baldr. Presumably, Frigg is identified with Hlín here because in this instance she failed to protect the one she loved, Baldr, as she will be unable to help Odin when Ragnarök comes.

Where Syn's protection is defensive, that of Hlín is more active. She fights for her favorites and spirits them out of danger. She protects against those who would take advantage of a woman's vulnerability as well as physical weakness. Her token is the blade or shield.

9. *Vár, who hears all oaths by the holy hearth.* Snorri tells us that Vár witnesses oaths and private contracts (*várar*), especially those between men and women, and punishes those who break them. Her name may also have some relationship to the English *ward*. Her functions are similar to those of the Greek Hestia, who lived in the hearthfire, heard all oaths, and received the first offering.

Vár's power lies in the words we use to make our vows or articulate our intentions. Through Vár, the word is the will, and affirmations acquire independent reality. She is especially concerned with those agreements that cannot be enforced by society, the unwritten commitments made by partners in a relationship and members of a family. Her symbol is the hearthfire or the oath ring.

10. *Vör, who knows all secrets.* Snorri tells us that Vör is "wise and enquiring, so that nothing can be concealed from her." Her name means "awareness," "the ability to find things out." She is the seereess of the group.

Vör is the power of knowing and keeping silence. In the outer world, she functions as the famous "woman's intuition," that is, the ability to interpret subtle clues to understand what is going on. On the inner planes, she is our guide to the unconscious. She reveals what is hidden and teaches us how to interpret the symbolic language of our dreams. She is seen in shadowy draperies, and her token is the dark veil.

11. *Snotra, the wise one, who always knows what to do.* Snotra is wise and courteous or gentle mannered. In Old Norse, *Snotr* is a name meaning "bride" or "lady," and for those who are considered wise or self-controlled.

Snotra's knowledge goes beyond mere etiquette. In

her we find the quality that enables one to surmount physical and social disasters. She has a profound understanding of human nature and social relationships. She not only understands the rules of conduct but also the reasons behind them. Her token is a linen handkerchief.

12. *Gná, the messenger.* Gná travels over sky and sea on a horse called Hoof-flourisher, carrying Frigg's messages throughout the worlds. Snorri says that her name means to soar or tower, but it may also be related to a word for the sound of a horse's neigh.

Gná is Frigg's power to transcend all worlds. She is freedom, the ability to soar beyond limitations. Through Gná, we communicate with the goddess and hear her replies. She appears radiant and vigorous, and her token is a statuette of a horse.

When honoring Frigg, you may deal with her alone, or you may set a circle of lights for her handmaidens around a central candle. The following is a poem for her:

> From the darkness of earth you arise, Fjorgvin's first daughter,
> Bending like the birch tree at the bounds of the glacier.
> You are the stillness at the heart of the world, you are its silence.
>
> Rams with white fleeces roam free round your dwelling:
> In your hall stands a loom; Norns spin the thread for your weaving.
> It is warped with the fates of the world. Only you see the pattern.

You sit at the head of the hearth, twelve maidens blaze
    around you,
Sparks spun from your brightness. In their faces you are re-
    flected;
You are all the women of all the worlds, you are the
    Beloved.

Giver of Law are you, and High Seat of Sovereignty.
All-father counsels kings, but it is you who choose them.
You teach magic to queens; you give names to the nations.

Golden the god you gave birth to, but Laufey's child
    betrayed him.
Your son will return when all else you love is ended,
all this you know, but you say nothing.

All-mother, around your altar now we are gathered,
Women together, wanting your wisdom,
Holy one hearken, hasten to help us.

Sing the following chant, substituting the name of one of the
handmaidens each time you repeat it:

Frigga [or Fulla, and so on] be welcome to our hall,
Gythja, oh hear us calling,
Beloved, to us we bid you blessings bring,
And hearken to our singing.

Sif

The goddess Sif is best known for her glorious golden hair.
Since in northern myth fair hair is the most important mark of

beauty, she is clearly among the fairest of the goddesses. Sif is the wife of Thor and mistress of his hall. By him she has a daughter called Thruth (or Trude), which means "strength," but by an earlier relationship she is the mother of Ullr, the god of winter and bow hunting. She is also stepmother to Thor's sons by Jarnsaxa. Her name comes from the Norse word for affinity or kinship by marriage rather than blood, and as matriarch of a composite family, she is an obvious goddess to bless step- and extended families of all kinds, and those who become sisters and brothers in a kindred.

The only story we have about Sif is the tale of how her hair was cut off by Loki. Whether he cut it to shame her after she slept with him, or whether he did it by stealth, the loss is devastating. For this reason, Sif is a powerful comforter and protector for those who have been raped, robbed, or abused physically or emotionally. Eventually, her hair is replaced by hair of real gold spun by the dwarves, but it will never be quite the same.

The cutting of Sif's hair is sometimes compared to the scything of the grain, whose gold it resembles, and Sif is honored as a goddess of the harvest. Her color is harvest gold, and we offer her wheat beer and barley cooked with honey and butter.

A prayer for Sif goes:

> Lovely lady golden fair,
> Combing blessings through your hair,
> Shining tresses softly flowing,
> As the wind through wheatfields blowing.
> Mighty mother of the strong,
> Guard the innocent from wrong,
> And when our lives by ill are stricken,
> Raise us up, that hope may quicken.
> All who've gathered here within,
> Welcome grant as clan and kin,
> Siblings by our own choice finding,
> Love and loyalty our binding.

And a song:

> In the waving wheat, we see you passing,
> We see your strength within the growing grain.
> Bright lady, be with us and bring us comfort,
> Sweet Sif, be near, and take away our pain.

Freyja

I first encountered Freyja when I was writing a novel about a young woman who comes into possession of Brisingamen, the sacred necklace of the goddess. At the time, I did not realize that I was opening the door not only to the goddess but also to all her friends. Freyja is not known as a separate goddess on the Continent, where Frigg is both goddess of love and queen. In the north, however, the two figures diverged. Her name means "lady" and may be an honorific used instead of older names.

Snorri tells us that Freyja survived all the other Aesir, which is not surprising, since medieval Christianity did not offer its converts a deity who would bless a healthy sexuality. Although Freyja is said to have had a husband, the mysterious Odh, he disappears from the scene early on, and though she mourns and searches for him, she also takes lovers where she will. It is possible that the Vanir cult had a somewhat more relaxed attitude toward sex than the Aesir did. When Loki accuses Freyja of having slept with every male at the feast, her father, Njordh, replies that he sees no reason a woman should not have a lover in addition to her husband ("Lokasenna": 33).

However, Freyja is much more than a sex goddess. She has one of the more impressive estates in Asgard. Her hall, Sessrumnir (the many-seated), is located in Folkvangar, the field full of folk. Besides the warriors whom she chooses, women may also end up there, as Egil Skallagrimsson's daughter proposed (*Egil's Saga*). So far as we know, the goddesses will survive Ragnarök. Freyja is a goddess of life, and we assume that she and her folk will play their part in building the new world.

Freyja's other major role is in magic. Indeed, her cult is a likely source for many of the traditions of English witchcraft. Snorri tells us that she taught the craft of seidh (see chapter 12) to the Aesir. Since Odin is also said to know seidh magic, it seems likely that Freyja was the one who taught it to him. The völva who prophesies from the seidh platform in the *Saga of Erik the Red* wears, among other things, a cap and gloves made from catskin, suggesting that she was a devotee of Freyja, since Freyja's chariot is drawn by cats.

The fact that the goddess can get two felines to work together is a proof of her power. She sometimes rides a boar called Hildisvini. She also has a falcon cloak that allows her to change shape and fly. Other animals associated with the goddess are the she-goat and the mare. Her greatest treasure is the necklace Brisingamen, whose price was a night spent with each of the four dwarves who crafted it. Such necklaces are often found on ancient figurines of goddesses, and this one seems to hold a great deal of the Lady's power. When she searched for Odh, she wept tears of gold, so that metal is associated with her, as is amber, the golden jewel that in Baltic lands comes from the sea. Today, the colors many associate with her are gold, green, and deep red.

Freyja's most popular title is "Vanadís," the "dís" or female guardian of the Vanir. Her bynames include Syr, Gefn, and Horn. Syr means "Sow," supporting the idea of the pig as a Vanic totem animal. Gefn is the same name as that of the Gefjun we find among Frigg's maidens, and the goddess who is said to have ploughed off the island of Zealand from the Swedish mainland and who may be viewed as the territorial goddess of Denmark. Hörn may come from a word for flax, so we can see Freyja making linen just as Frigg spins wool. It seems likely that the goddess of prosperity was worshipped in many districts under different names, but all shared the title of "Lady." Kveldulf Gundarsson proposes "the Frowe" as a Germanic version of the name. Like her twin brother, Freyr, she is invoked for productivity of all kinds, which in the old days usually involved fertility. So when you are asking her help, be very precise about just what kind of productivity you have in mind.

Offerings for Freyja include barley, pork, honey and other sweets, and sweet drinks such as apricot ale and, of course, goldwasser. Next to Odin, Freyja seems to be the Norse deity who is most likely to spontaneously appear in people's lives. Her splendid, joyous energy makes her one of the most popular of the goddesses.

The following is the prayer I wrote for her in *Brisingamen*:

> Hail Freyja! All hail to the goddess,
> Highest and holiest, hail!
> Brisingamen's bearer, Bride of the Vanir,
> We boldly bespeak thee here.
> Gefn the giver, gold-bright goddess,
> Grant us thy favor now.
> There where thou sittest in splendid Sessrumnir;
> Linen-clothed Lady of Love.
> As Syr we salute thee, Hildisvini's rider,
> Boar-Ottar's savior art thou.
> Gullveig the golden, fast bound in the flames,
> Reforged thee thy fate in the fire.
> Mardöll of the waters, mighty thy beauty,
> Mistress of gods and men;
> Mare of the Vanir, as Gondul dost thou gallop,
> Bearing kings from the battlefield.
> Lady of life, light dost thou kindle—
> Goddess, show us thy glory!

And a song:

> You lead the dance among the witches,
> You bring the people joy and riches,

Radiant lady, ever dear,
Freyja, hasten to us here!

Nerthus

If Freyja is known only in Scandinavia, our only source for
Nerthus is found in the *Germania*, written by the first-century
Roman author Tacitus. The name, and as we shall see, her function,
is close enough to the Germanic *Erde* ("earth"), to support identification of Nerthus as a goddess of earth's fertility. Its similarity to the
name "Njorth" also suggests an original brother-sister pair, although
this cannot be proven. It should be noted that for the early Europeans, the separation between earth and water was not so distinct as
it is in modern paganism, especially along the marshy coasts of the
North Sea.

According to Tacitus, Nerthus was worshipped by a people called
the Ingvaeones, whose name is related to one of the names for Freyr.
Her shrine was on an island in the ocean. At the beginning of the
planting season, her priests would bring the image to the mainland
and set it, veiled, in a cart drawn by oxen. Wherever the cart passed,
everyone would put away their weapons and keep the peace for the
duration of the festival.

Such processions are known from other sources in Germanic history, especially for Vanic deities, and are still a part of folk religion in
many cultures, from Shinto Japan to Roman Catholic Italy. In the
Flateyjarbók, we are told of a similar custom in which the deity being
transported is Freyr. Tacitus goes on to tell us that when the progress
of the goddess was complete, her image was taken back to its shrine,
where it was ceremonially washed by two slaves who were afterward
drowned.

Today, several images of Nerthus have been made, one of
which is at the Brushwood Folklore Center in New York, where

it is carried around the campground at the beginning of the
Starwood Festival. The image is kept veiled. No one is drowned
after handling it, but when one of the other images was un-
veiled at Trothmoot, everyone was immediately drenched by
rain.

Nerthus fills the "earth goddess" niche in the Germanic pantheon
and is one of the northern goddesses who is most accessible to the
greater pagan community.

The following is a prayer I wrote for her:

> Erce, Erce, Erce, Eorthan Modir,
> Rooted, we reach for ancient wisdom,
> Strength we draw from sacred soil.
> Nerthus, now our need is near us,
> Honor we offer—a holy harvest
> Bring forth in beauty, Bride and Mother—
> Goodly gifts for the kin of Ríg.

And the song we sing as we bear the goddess in her wagon around
the field at Starwood:

> She is coming, she is coming
> From the depths of the earth,
> She is coming from her island in the sea.
> She is coming, she is coming
> Bringing joy, bringing mirth,
> She is coming to set us free!

Hella

Some may be surprised to see Hella listed among the goddesses,
and yet although she is a shadowy figure in the lore, she has become

an important deity to a number of heathens today. There is a sense in which she plays a role similar to that of Idunn, with whom we began this chapter. As Idunn brings renewal in the world of the gods, Hella guards the ancestors whose folkways we are trying to restore. Together, they provide us with a connection to all aspects of the past.

Hella is the daughter of Loki by the giantess Angrbodha. When the gods decided how to deal with Loki's strange offspring, she was given the world farthest beneath the roots of the World Tree as her domain. There she is required to offer "board and lodging" to all those who die of sickness or old age (*Edda,* ch. 34). Snorri also tells us that she is half black and half flesh colored and looks "rather grim and gloomy." It is not made clear which half is which, but today many see her divided down the middle, dark on one side and white (or even skeletal) on the other.

As we will see in chapter 11, the Germanic peoples believed the dead had a number of options, of which going to Hella's realm is only one. Although it is the Germanic underworld, those who have visited it in visions find that we may also contact the nonheathen dead there. Hella gives peace and rest after the troubles of the world. In her realm one can access the accumulated wisdom of the ages and find the answers to many questions.

Offerings for Hella tend to be dark and bitter, such as black bread, stout, or a very dry zinfandel wine. Her colors, of course, are black and white. Some heathens honor her when other pagans are celebrating Samhain, since it is a time when many ancestors are being called and the doors are open between the worlds.

The following is a prayer to invoke Hella:

> Queen of Darkness, Loki's daughter,
> Hella, when we seek thy hallows,
> Bless us with thy bright face, lady,
> Show a pathway through the shadows.
> Where the ancestors are biding,

Where all memories are hiding,
To thy mercy now confiding,
Hella, we hail thee now.

And a song:

Lady of the Darkness,
Ruler of the night,
We sleep within thy shadows
To wake into thy light.

CHAPTER 8

Ways of Devotion

People are still congratulating Dave and Sofia when Karen bears the horn to Liliane, a strong, no-nonsense type whose day job is as a bank executive. Her subordinates would never recognize the anxiety she shows now to her friends.

Holding the horn, she looks around the room.

"Most of you know that my husband's in the Army Reserves. Well, he got called up last week and has already left for training. They need people with his specialty, and he'll be deployed soon. So I want to lift this horn to Tyr. Wolf-binder, I ask you to keep my husband safe. But even more," her voice cracks, "I ask that you be with him and help him walk the path of honor, to see what's right and do it no matter how hard it may be. Bring him back to me, lord, and I will make a feast for you that people here will be talking about for years to come. Hail Tyr!"

The murmur of shock and sympathy swells as she drinks and hands the horn back to Karen.

"You notice she didn't require him to bring Gabe back with all his body parts still in place," mutters Thorolf.

"No—only his honor," his wife answers him. "She called on Tyr, and his first concern is justice. In her place, I would be asking Thor to keep his hammer between you and harm every minute of every day."

"Do you think she's wrong?" Thorolf asks, and she knows he is wondering if it's his responsibility as gothi to do some counseling.

"I think it's between them and the gods."

"Ásatrú" means the troth of the Aesir. For today's heathens, the core of the religion is our relationship with our goddesses and gods. But how are we to honor them? Even if our ancestors could have imagined such a thing as a *Book of Common Prayer*, it is unlikely that we would be able to follow it exactly as written. However, as "reconstructionist" pagans, we are committed to restoring as much of the old ways as we can. Fortunately, the lore tells us when the seasonal rites were celebrated and gives some hints about what they did. On that foundation, we are building a new heathen tradition that continues to evolve.

Friends of the Gods

Perhaps because we have been such a peripatetic population, most North American heathens find it easier to make a strong connection to the gods and goddesses than to the ancestors or spirits of the land. Although not all of our deities are mentioned in the lore of both the Continent and Scandinavia, the principal gods and goddessses are found in both areas, and Theodsmen who call the gods by their Anglo-Saxon names can share a sumble with followers of Scandinavian Ásatrú. The sumble itself, a ritual in which the horn is passed so that participants may drink to the gods, heroes, and others, is another tradition that virtually all heathens share. For more about this, see chapter 12.

Heathens may differ, however, in their ideas about what the gods are. Perhaps the most widely held belief is that they are spiritual beings who exist in another dimension of reality that intersects our own. There are also those who believe that the gods have a physical existence in another universe, from which they contact us. For others, they are culture-specific examples of archetypal figures (Thor is seen as an aspect of the thunder god, while Loki is grouped with the tricksters, and so on). For most, I suspect, the important question is not what the gods are, but whether they will answer when we call on them.

Although I have worked successfully with individual deities from a number of other cultures, I have found that as a group, the Germanic pantheon is the most "alive, well, and eager to party." Whether this is because they were the last to be worshipped in Europe before the conversion to Christianity, or because they belong to the culture from which our language and many of our institutions come, I do not know, but it is my experience that even obscure Germanic deities make their presence felt when we call on them. And when they do respond, it is as comrades and allies who want to work with us rather than as overlords who desire slaves.

The old Viking concept of "friendship" with the gods characterizes the relationship many heathens have with their deities today. In *Eyrbyggjasaga*, Thorolf Mostur-Beard is described as "a close friend of Thor." In Norway, he was in charge of Thor's temple on Mostur Island. When he ran into trouble with the king, he asked Thor what to do and was advised to go to Iceland. When he made landfall, he threw the pillars of the high seat from the temple overboard and claimed the land where the god caused them to float ashore. In *Gisli's Saga*, a man called Thorgrim was a "friend of Freyr," so beloved by the god that after his death snow never stayed on his grave mound because the god was unwilling to have frost come between them.

Friendship provides a useful model for our relationship with the gods and goddesses and other wights. Like any other relationship, friendship with a god requires mutual respect and attention. We talk to our deities, share our food and drink with them, and quiet our minds so that we can hear what they have to say. For some, these relationships become extremely close and last life-long, while others may work closely with one god for a time, and then be "passed on" to another. Still others may maintain less intense relationships with a number of deities.

Although most kindreds try to make sure that all the gods and goddesses are honored, in any group there will probably be several members who are known for their devotion to specific gods. Of these, Thor and Odin are probably the most popular (or perhaps the most active in recruiting) followed closely by Tyr and Freyr. Among the goddesses, Freyja and Frigg both claim enthusiastic followers. Although it is more common for men to find patron gods and women, goddesses, Odin has many female devotees, and I know of several priests of Freyja. Someone who is especially devoted may become known as a "Thorsman" or a "Freyjaswoman" (or, of course, a "Thorswoman" or a "Freyjasman").

Just as friendship comes in different degrees, so does the intensity of devotion to one's god. For most, the relationship remains at the level of admiration and companionship, but for some the connection approaches the intensity and commitment of a marriage. Even those who are not so devoted may at times experience the presence of one of the gods or goddesses with the same overwhelming power as mystics in other religions do.

Offerings

In the "Havamál": 144, we are asked if we know how to "bid," how to "send," and how to "offer." Bidding means to address, to pray. The *blót* is the ceremony in which the offering is made and the people blessed (see the discussion later in this chapter). The offering must then be sent to the gods. In return, they reach out to us with their help and love. The process is reciprocal. However, offerings should be kept in proportion. The High One also tells us that:

> 'Tis better not to pray than to make too many offerings,
>   One gift demands another.
> It's better not to send than to sacrifice too much. (145)

In the old days, a sacrifice was literally that—something of value, usually an animal, that was ritually killed and "given" to the god. This practice was universal in the ancient world, and in most cases was quite practical. The blood would be poured over the altar and sprinkled in blessing, and the head and hide hung up and left as an offering, but the meat was cooked and shared out among the worshippers. The only time many of the poorer folk got meat would be at the festivals. The idea that it is better to eat only animals that have been blessed and killed humanely in a religious context survives today in kosher and halal butchering. However, to do the job badly is the reverse of holy, and since few modern heathens have the requisite skill, our festal food usually comes from the grocery store.

Today, heathens offer drink and already cooked food, and rather than blessing each other with drops of blood, we pour a little mead into the offering bowl. Since we no longer count our wealth on the hoof, it is the cut of meat and the age of the drink that determine the expense, and thus how much of a "sacrifice" it will be to offer it. A selection of items from the feast may be set outside or burned in the fireplace. Drink is offered as we toast the gods.

However there are times when we feel the need to make a sacrifice that we will not also share. Both the Celtic and Germanic peoples sometimes deposited captured weapons and treasure in lakes or marshes as a thank-offering for victory. The contemporary practice of throwing coins into pools, fountains, or almost any body of water while making a wish may hark back to this tradition. I have seen a modern heathen cast a very nice replica sword (first ceremonially "killed" by bending it) into a lake. I trust it was appreciated by the gods—the gift certainly impressed those who witnessed the offering.

Prayer

Friendship with the gods, like our relationships with other humans, is maintained by regular communication. There has been a lot of discussion regarding the stance in which we should address our gods. While some hold that a heathen should always stand upright when invoking and face the deities from a position that, if not equal, at least displays a spirit of independence, the Arab chronicler Ibn Fadlan reports that the Rus traders on the Volga bowed down before the godposts where they had made their offerings. Our word *worship* comes from the Old English *weordhscipe*, which means to "give worth" to something by honoring it. What must come first is the attitude we bring to worship. The old saying that you should "put yourself in an attitude of prayer and you will find that you are praying" reminds us that the details of practice are important mainly insofar as they help us to reach a state of mind in which we can make contact with the gods. (For a further discussion of these ideas, see "Worshipping the Gods" at www.hrafnar.org/norse/worship.html., or *Our Troth* Vol II.

The prayer itself can be a silent outpouring from the heart or a formal invocation. Praying out loud is usually part of a group ritual. Using traditional forms such as Anglo-Saxon four-beat alliterative verse for prayers may not make a difference to the gods, but choosing an appropriate form does help the human listeners. A traditional format goes as follows:

> Hail [best-known name of the deity and a descriptive epithet]
> Child of [parent, if known], lover of [spouse, if known],

You who dwell in [hall]
You did [summarize one or more of the deity's deeds]
With your [characteristic tool or weapon]
Come swiftly to aid me [or, Come and be with us]
As I [summarize situation or problem].

For examples of such invocations, see the sections on the gods and goddesses in chapters 6 and 7. Formal prayers are usually read or memorized. An extemporaneous and conversational address is more intimate and can be equally effective.

The best-known prayer from the lore is the verse that the valkyrie Sigdrifa speaks after being awakened from her magic sleep by Sigurd. A rhymed translation goes:

Hail to thee Day, and Day's bright boy,
Hail to the Night and her daughter's joy.
With eyes that bless us, may you see,
And grant to those here, victory.
The goddesses and gods we call
And holy earth, who gives to all—
Give us here wise words and weal,
And in this life, the hands that heal! ("Lay of Sigdrifa": 2)

Or you may prefer to use the version in Lee Hollander's 1962 translation of the *Elder Edda*.

Not all prayer is done in public or aloud. In meditation, one can journey to the homes of the gods to observe, to learn, and to ask questions. We also talk to our divine friends when we are in more ordinary states of consciousness and often "hear" them answering. As long as these conversations are not audible to others, this should not be a problem. It is also permissible to argue with the gods—in fact, they seem to prefer people to stand up to them. If, for instance, Freyja gives you to understand that she would really like a golden cup for her altar, you are perfectly justified in asking her to provide the gold so that you can buy it.

Your home altar can provide a useful focus for meditation. Light the candle, pour a little mead into the offering cup, and sit back where you can contemplate the image. You may find it helpful to play some music that reminds you of the god or goddess with whom you are working. Breathe slowly and quietly; let your body relax. Gaze at the image, or build up a picture of the deity in your mind, and then close your eyes. Holding the image, open your awareness and articulate your question or need (which may be as simple as a desire for contact) and sit quietly, waiting. Don't worry if distracting thoughts intrude—recognize them, and then let them go. You may have a sense of the presence of the god or goddess, an answer or idea may come into your mind, or you may simply find the quiet time relaxing. Even if nothing seems to be happening, one sometimes later finds that there has been a change.

Altars

A heathen altar can range from a section of mantelpiece where you keep your Thor's hammer and drinking horn to a table dedicated to a particular deity. A table altar may also be created for a ritual. The simplest outdoor altar is a pile of stones. Statues of Norse gods and goddesses are becoming available from Sacred Source (see the resources section) and other vendors, but it is just as appropriate, and even more authentic, to carve a face into a piece of wood.

The altar for a blót in honor of a specific deity is usually both larger and simpler. On a cloth of a color appropriate to the deity, one sets the drinking horn, offering bowl, and bottles of the liquid that is to be drunk, and whatever other items will be used in the ritual. Sometimes there will be room for candles, flowers, and an image, or a picture or banner can be hung behind the table.

A simple home altar might start with a piece of colored cloth, on which one places a statue or picture of the deity, some of the deity's symbols, a horn, goblet or bowl for drink offerings, a candle, and perhaps a vase for greenery or flowers. See the table on pages 74–75 for suggested colors for different deities. If your altar will honor more than one god, a white or natural-colored cloth or placemat may be best. You can edge it with ornamental braid, or embroider a verse in runes around the border. Home altars can be protected from small children and animals by placing them on high shelves or covering them with a cloth. A temporary outdoor altar can be made by heaping up stones or a permanent one by cementing them together.

Blót

In the lore, the word *blót* (pronounced "bloat") refers to a feast and/or a sacrifice at which we offer gifts to the gods. In the Viking Age, the animals brought to the feast were sacrificed and the people blessed with the blood, which conveyed to them some of the power of the gods. While the meat was cooking, the chief of the feast blessed it and then the horn of mead or ale. This was followed by a sumble, as described later on, in which the cup or horn was blessed, probably with the sign of the hammer, and in successive rounds, gods, heroes, and ancestors received a toast or a prayer. This was followed by the feast.

Today, the blót has become one of the most generally accepted heathen practices. Although inspired by the traditional procedure, the blót is now generally a ritual with a specific focus such as honoring a god or goddess or celebrating a holiday. Ritual style varies from kindred to kindred, with some groups favoring a rather precise structure while others are extremely informal. Regardless, the style and content should be tailored to the people and purpose in question. The essence of the process is exchange—our attention and energy, symbolized by the offerings, for the help and blessings of the gods.

In the *Book of Blóts* (2004, 16), Rod Landreth lists the main types of rituals as: celebratory rites that honor an event such as the turning of the season; "folk-binding" rites that strengthen the community; goal-driven rites performed to achieve a specific purpose; initiatory rites such as joining a kindred; and devotional rites that bring us closer to the gods and goddesses. As he points out, in some blóts several purposes may be combined.

A number of outlines for blóts have been proposed. Most agree on the following elements:

1. *Preparation*: This stage includes everything from setting up the altar to gathering the participants. They usually stand, or if a feast will follow, sit in a circle or oval. If the rite is not taking place in a dedicated space, the leader may want to ward it, either beforehand or as a part of the ceremony. Even if warding is not needed, to ceremonially define the boundaries of the ritual space can help participants to focus. Many groups use the Hammer Rite created by Edred Thorsson (1984, 91). Another method inspired by traditional practice is to carry fire around the circle or to inscribe it with a spear. Some feel that this stage should also include an offering to the spirit of the house or land.

2. *Focusing*: Either before beginning or at this point, the leader should explain to the group what the purpose of the blót will be and summarize what will be going on. Once the rite has begun, it may be useful to include an appropriate reading from the lore.

3. *Invocation*: Also known as the Call, Halsing, or Bidding—this is the prayer that welcomes the god or gods to the gathering. A prayer may follow the format given earlier, you may write something like those given in the chapters on gods and goddesses, or you may speak as the spirit moves you. Writing such prayers in a Germanic style will intensify the focus and be perceived as more authentic than using ordinary English prose.

4. *Offering*: Giving a gift to the god or gods. In some blóts, the offering consists of the mead or other drink, which at this point is consecrated to the deity, followed by the blessing. However, depending on the purpose of the ritual, the offering might also consist of some action, from a ritual drama based on one of the myths to the blessing and burial of a bread image. In that case, the drink would be blessed following the other offerings. The actual consecration consists of a spoken blessing and the "signing" of the horn with the hammer sign or a rune.

5. *Blessing*: Once the drink has been blessed, a little is poured into the offering bowl. Some prefer to have some water already in the bowl to dilute the liquor (especially if you are using wine) to spare people's clothing. Using a sprig of greenery (the *hlaut-teinn)* as an asperger, the leader or an assistant sprinkles the hallowed liquid on the altar and on each participant, thus blessing them with the might of the gods. The Theodish traditions have a particularly beautiful ceremony for this.

6. *Sharing*:   The horn is now passed around the circle. In some groups it is passed from hand to hand. In others, a designated valkyrie receives the horn and hands it to the next

participant. The person receiving the horn usually lifts it to honor the deity and then says "Hail [Name]" and/or a few words of prayer or praise, then drinks (the physics of drinking horns make it advisable to drink with the point of the horn turned down to avoid getting splashed) and hands it back or passes it on. When everyone has drunk, any liquid remaining is poured into the offering bowl. If the rite is being held outdoors, this may be poured out on the earth immediately. Indoors, it may be carried out immediately or after the ritual.

7. *Completion*: When the business of the blót is over, the feasting may begin, or the area desanctified and the participants allowed to depart.

For a more detailed discussion of blóts, with many examples in various styles, see the Troth's *Book of Blóts* (2004).

Sumble

The passages with which each chapter in this book begins are part of a *sumble* (Old English *symbel*), the ritual that is most basic to Heathenry and most widely practiced. In the custom of toasting people at wedding and funeral receptions, it remains a part of our culture to this day. The sumble can take place as a single round within the context of a blót, or it can stand alone as a ceremony. In sumble, the mead or ale is drunk to remember those who are worthy of honor and to proclaim the deeds for which we hope people will remember us.

The Icelandic-style sumble consists of three rounds. In the first round, each person offers a prayer, oath, or praise to the god or goddess of his or her choice. In the second round, we remember heroes and the dead. The third is usually an open round in which people may honor the living, including those present. This is also usually the round in which boasts and oaths are made. In the Anglo-Saxon style, the rounds continue until the sumble leader feels the ritual has reached a climax.

Some feel that sumble should only take place under a roof, while others have no problem with holding it outdoors. In either case, participants sit in a circle. The sumble leader (usually the leader of the group or a distinguished guest) acts as master or mistress of ceremonies, announcing the focus of the round, and filling and blessing the horn. In the Anglo-Saxon style, a woman, designated the valkyrie, may be chosen to bear the horn to each participant, or each guest may have his or her own horn or goblet. The horn may also be passed from hand to hand. In an open-ended sumble, some kindreds allow anyone who feels the need to call for a "water horn" to be circulated between rounds. Those who for any reason cannot or should not drink may honor the horn by kissing it, pouring a little on the earth if outdoors or into the offering bowl, or dabbing a drop on their forehead. Some kindreds may supply a second sumble horn filled with a nonalcoholic drink such as apple juice.

Participants may speak sitting or standing. Some may choose simply to honor the horn in silence. Since oaths taken in sumble not only affect the fate of the one making them but also that of all those who bear witness, in an Anglo-Saxon-style sumble, a *thyle*, or speaker, challenges oaths he or she thinks impossible, unwise, or likely to bring bad luck, and advises on ways to improve them. The thyle may require the speaker to say what compensation he or she will pay if the boast is not fulfilled. The most serious oaths may be sworn on an arm ring kept for that purpose by the kindred. What is said in sumble is recorded in the Well of Wyrd and should be treated accordingly. A properly conducted sumble creates an atmosphere of communion between members of the group and the gods.

Heathen Holy Days

In the sagas, we hear of feasts at the beginning of winter, Yule, and spring. Folklore attests to midsummer festivals as well. In addition, a number of other observances are mentioned, though not all of them are understood very well. Today, most kindreds observe the seasonal blessings and pick and choose among the additional possibilities for their other meetings during the year. The following list has been compiled from a number of sources on the Web and elsewhere. Not all groups observe the days that honor heathen heroes and martyrs. Kindreds observe these feasts in many different ways, but those holidays that most groups celebrate in some way are marked with a valknut, ⩘.

WINTER

In the north, winter starts early. Just as sunset marked the beginning of a day, winter's period of gestation began the year.

⩘ First full moon after the fall equinox: Winter Finding (*Winter Fylleth*) or Winter Nights (*Vetmaettr*). The Ásatrú Alliance separates these holidays, observing Winter Finding on the equinox in September and Winter Nights in October. The old Icelandic calendar put it between October 11 and 17. Others favor October 12. Sigvat, an eleventh-century Christian skald, complained in a poem about having been refused hospitality at a farm because the people were sacrificing to the alfar. The alfar (elves) are ancestral spirits. When only the female ancestors are meant, the term *dísir* is used. Many kindreds use this holiday to honor the ancestors and celebrate the harvest. Some honor only the dísir, while others follow a Norwegian tradition and honor the alfar in the fall and the dísir in February.

October 8 or 28—Erik the Red's Day, honoring the founder of the Greenland colony.

October 9 or Columbus Day—Leif Eriksson's Day, honoring the

first European to actually live in North America at the settlement at L'Anse aux Meadows, Newfoundland.

November 9—Queen Sigrid's Day. Sigrid was married first to the old king of Sweden, and left him when she found out she was expected to commit suttee when he died. Olaf Tryggvason courted her, but insisted she become Christian. When she replied that she didn't mind what gods he worshipped, but she herself would stick with the gods of her family, he slapped her and called her a heathen bitch. Later, she married King Svein Forkbeard of Denmark and incited him to bring Olaf down.

⛊ November 11 or Veteran's Day—Feast of the Einherjar. Many kindreds take this opportunity to honor the warriors in Odin's hall and by extension all those who fall defending their country.

November 25, 27, or Thanksgiving Day—Hunters' Holiday. Offerings are made to Ullr and Skadhi for help during the hunting season. Those who stay home on Thanksgiving celebrate the day as a family festival with a special offering to the house wight.

December 9—Egil Skallagrimsson's Day. A time to honor the grouchy berserker who was also one of the greatest poets of his age. Read *Egil's Saga*. Try your hand at writing poetry.

YULE MONTH

December 13—Santa Lucia's Day/Feast of Sunna. This feast, in which Sunna's role has been transferred to an Italian saint and moved from its original solstice date, is still a national holiday in Sweden. The eldest daughter of the house, robed in white and crowned with candles, rises and serves coffee and sun cakes to the family.

December 14—Tulya's E'en. This day opens what the people of the Shetland Islands, whose culture was primarily Norse, called the "Merry Month." Seven days before Yule, all the trolls are released from underground. This is also the season when Odin and the Wild Hunt (*oskerei*) ride. Householders protect their farms by *saining* ("blessing") them with the sign of the hammer, and fire is carried through all the buildings.

December 16 or Thursday before Yule—Tunderman's Night. All work is suspended, especially that involving wheels. The Yuletide fuel supply is brought in. Take this opportunity to have a feast honoring Thor and ask his protection from winter's storms.

⚄ December 19—Mother Night. A feast in honor of Frigg and mothers. A time to celebrate the family, especially the women and children, and female ancestors. Eat Yule cookies and read fairy tales. (Celebrated in the Shetlands on the 15 as "Helya's E'en.") From this time through the end of Yule, all spinning must be finished and put away.

⚄ December 20 (or the eve of the solstice)—Yule Eve. The longest night of the year. Light the Yule log. Bake Yule cakes for each child. The house must be thoroughly cleaned and a light left burning all night. Put out a bowl of porridge with a pat of butter on top for the house wight.

⚄ December 21 (sometimes celebrated on the 25 to coincide with Christmas)—Yule. The Yule feast is held, featuring a very large pork roast in honor of Freyr. At this time the holiest oaths are sworn. Masquers representing the Wild Hunt may pay a visit to households. An offering may be put out for the oskerei.

December 31 (or January 5)—Perchta's Night. The goddess of women's work (also known as Holda) visits houses to make sure all the work is done. Eat oatmeal and herring in her honor.

January 1 (or 6)—Threttándi (Thirteenth Night). The liminal moment between the old and new years when oaths are most powerful. Make a start on the work you want to accomplish during the year. This is also a good time to do rune readings for the coming year.

January 9—Raud the Strong's Day. Put to death by Olaf Digre for refusing to convert.

January 11 (or twenty-four nights after Yule)—Up-Helly-Aa. A time for bonfires, protection rituals of all kinds, and dancing. At midnight, bang on pots and drums and chase the trolls back into their holes.

January 17–25—Thorrablót. An Icelandic holiday in honor of

Old Man Winter, at which traditional winter-preserved food is eaten, washed down with lots of alcohol. North American heathens generally celebrate it in honor of Thor.

February 2 (or the date on which working the ground becomes possible in your area)—Charming of the Plow. Offerings are made to Mother Earth and the first furrow is cut. Feast of Barri, celebrating the marriage of Freyr and Gerd. Plant seeds indoors for later transplanting.

February 2 or 14—Idis-thing (Disting or Dísablót). If the female ancestors were not honored at Winter Nights, they may be celebrated with their own feast when winter is beginning to give way to spring.

February 14—Feast of Vali. Ascribed to Vali, who avenged Baldr, probably because of the similarity of the name to Valentine. A celebration of the returning light, of romance, and of marriage.

March 9—Olver the Martyr's Day. Killed by Olaf Digre while preparing for the spring sacrifice.

SUMMER

▲ March 20, spring equinox, or the first full moon after the equinox—Ostara, Sigrblót, or Sumarmál (celebrated separately by some on April 17 or 19). This feast was held to open the summer half of the year. In Viking times, the king sacrificed for victory during the coming campaigns, and farmers made offerings for the growth of the crops. Today, most heathens draw on continental German traditions of the goddess Ostara or Eostre (who gave her name to Easter), complete with rabbits and eggs, to celebrate the rebirth of Nature.

April 9, Jarl Hakon's Day. Hakon Sigurdsson, the Jarl of Hladhir, temporarily reversed the tide of Christianization and Europeanization in Norway, helping the old ways to survive.

April 23, or Earth Day—Yggdrasil Day. As descendants of the ash and elm, this is a time to honor our kinship with and responsibility to care for the forests of the world.

▲ April 30 and May 1—Walpurgisnacht (Waluberga's Eve) and

May Day. A festival celebrating the flowering of spring. On May eve, the old powers revel on the Brocken and other holy mountains. It is a good time for magical workings. May Day is a time to rejoice in the springtide and honor Freyja and the Vanir.

May 9—Gudrod's Day. Gudrod was martyred for opposing Olaf Tryggvason by having his tongue cut out.

June 8—Lindisfarne Day. Anniversary of the first Viking raid and the beginning of the Viking Age.

June 9—Sigurd the Volsung's Day. Sigurd (Siegfried) is the hero of the greatest of the Germanic epics and inspiration for Richard Wagner's *Ring* operas.

⬧ June 21 or summer solstice—Midsummer. Celebration in honor of summer's growth, taking advantage of the opportunity to party outdoors all night with lots of food and drink. A time to honor Sunna or Baldr.

July 9—Day of Unn the Deep-Minded. A great matriarch and early settler of Iceland.

August 9—Radbod of Frisia's Day. Radbod refused baptism when informed he would be separated from his ancestors in the afterlife.

August 21 (or August 1 in more southern areas)—Freyfaxi or Loaf-fest. Beginning of the harvest and first loaf from the new grain, celebrated with sports and horse racing in honor of Freyr or Thor and Sif.

September 9—Arminius Day. In this month, Arminius (Hermann) of the Cherusci trapped and destroyed three Roman legions in the Teutoburger Wald, thus keeping the Romans from conquering east of the Rhine.

Rites of Passage

The major rites of passage celebrated by heathens include the blessing of children, coming-of-age rituals for adolescents, marriage, memorial services, and rites of affiliation. A baby blessing usually includes formally accepting the newborn into the family, sprinkling his or her head with water (a heathen rite before it was adopted by Christians, who previously had baptized by total immersion), and giving it a name. Man- and woman-making rites may include an ordeal or test of some kind in addition to gift giving and a formal welcome as an adult member of the community. Heathen wedding ceremonies generally feature a marriage contract and boasting of the qualities of bride and groom by their families and friends. At memorial services, guests drink to the departed and feast in his or her honor. All these, of course, also include asking blessings from the goddesses and gods.

In addition, kindreds often have formal rituals for becoming a member. Not all heathens feel the need to make a formal renunciation of their previous faith, but many do so and follow it with a self-dedication to the Aesir. Unfortunately, space does not allow me to include the actual rituals here. For examples of these, as well as for many other types of blóts and rites, see the Troth's *Book of Blóts* (2004) and volume two of Kveldulf Gundarsson's *Our Troth* (2005).

Mythic Dramas

A final class of heathen ritual is the mythic drama. The *Eddas* are a treasure house of good stories that lend themselves to dramatic treatment as part of a seasonal celebration. Many of the poems in the *Elder Edda* are already in the form of a dialogue and need very little additional work to turn into plays. Some possibilities include:

Springtime: The marriage of Freyr and Gerd (based on the
    "Lay of Skirnir")
    The courtship of Mengloth (based on the "Lay of
    Svipsdag")

Summer: Thor's wedding (based on the "Lay of Thrym")
    The fatherhood of Ríg (based on the "Lay of Ríg")

Winter: Baldr's drama (based on the "Dream of Baldr")

CHAPTER 9

Germanic Magic

Ingleif is sitting next to Liliane. He is young, blond, and good looking. As he gets up to take the horn, the bells hanging from his belt jingle faintly.

"As most of you know, I'm a Freyrsman, but tonight I am going to offer the horn to Freyr's sister, who taught seidh magic to the Aesir and who I hope will teach it to me. I've studied the shamanic practices of other cultures, but there's a lot of magic in the Northern tradition, and I think our kindred should have someone who understands it.

"Freyja, Freyja, fair one, hear me!
Gydhja, guide me well each day,
Vanadís, reveal the vision,
As to Odin, you opened the way.
Freyja, Freyja, fair one, follow,
In your falcon form wing free,
Ottar's rider, fate's road showing,
As with seidh sight I learn to see."

He raises the horn with a flourish and drinks deep.

Although magical workings are not central to Heathenry in the same way that they are to Wicca, they are an important part of the Germanic spiritual tradition. Today, Germanic magic is often divided into two major categories: *galdr*, consisting of all kinds of magic involving speech or song, and *seidhr*, sometimes called "mind magic," which includes techniques involving trance and folk magic. It is important to note, however, that unlike Wicca, which is as much a magical as a religious tradition, Ásatrú focuses on folkways and religious practice in which magic plays a minor part.

Magic Workers

Historically, in the Germanic countries magic was with a few exceptions not a full-time profession. However, like music and poetry, it was a specialty that many might practice part of the time. In each community certain individuals would gain a reputation for expertise in various kinds of magical work. The rich magical vocabulary of the Germanic languages shows just how varied this work could be. Where we must make do with *magic, witchcraft, wizardry, sorcery* or *woo woo*, Old English magical terms include *scinn*, a phantom or illusion, as in *scinn-craeft, galdor-craeft* for spell work, *wicce-craeft* (witchery), *lyb-craeft* (drug-based witchery), *wigle* (divination), *bealo-craeft* (evil art), and *tungol-craeft* (star lore).

Richard Cleasby and Gudbrand Vigfusson's *An Icelandic-English Dictionary* (1874) gives us the term *völva* for a "prophetess, sibyl, or wisewoman," which was applied to many notable figures in the sagas, as well as to the speaker of "Völuspá." *Thul* (or the Old English *thyle*) is a title for a "wiseman," a sage or bard who sits at the *pulr-stoll*—the "seat of thul" ("Havamál": 111) to speak or sing. A woman who practices seidhr is a *seidhkona* or *spákona*. A male practitioner is a *seidhmadhr* or *spámadhrmadhr*. A *vitki* (Old English *witiga*) is a "wizard." Older masculine and feminine forms may be *veitaga* and *veitago*.

The verb *vitka* means "to bewitch." Other names include Old Norse *rúna-meistari* (rune master) and *galdra-meistari* or *galdra-kona* (a man or woman who uses spells). Less complimentary terms include *trollkjerring* for those who deal with uncanny wights and *fjölkunnig* for one who is skilled in the black arts (this may be related to the later English term *cunning man*). Then there was Geirrid Thorolf's daughter, of whom it was sufficient to say that she was "a woman who knew a thing or two." (*Eyrbyggjasaga*, p. 45). Although the seidh workers seem to have been professionals who went from place to place, most of those who practiced Norse magic were apparently farmers (or in the case of Egil Skallagrimsson, a skald and warrior) or housewives for whom magic was a sideline.

Gand

The closest we can come to a general term for magic in Old Norse is *gand*, which can be found in compounds for magical beings and objects or activities associated with magic workers. It may be defined as the art of using an object, such as a wand, staff, or broom to channel magical power. The *nidstöng*, or scorn pole, described in *Egilsaga* was a post carved with a curse in runes on which the head of a horse or other animal was set to frighten away the land spirits from the one being cursed. This practice was also known as *hopt*.

Galdr

The word *galdr* (Old English *galdor*) means a song or spell, but is also used in compounds for other magical practices or items, presumably because spells are chanted when using them. As a magical term, it is comparable to the English words we derive from the Latin *cantare*, such as *enchant* and *incantation*. Galdr is considered by many today to cover all kinds of verbal and ceremonial magic, as opposed to the mind magic of seidh. In practice, of course, most magical workings require words, actions, and a change in consciousness, so the point may be moot.

There is some evidence that spells were sung in a high voice. They were used to bind or to loose bindings, to enchant, daze, and enthrall. Compounds indicate the variety of spells:

Val-galdr: waking the dead to learn from them (by verbal summoning or by carving runes on an alder chip and placing it under the tongue of the corpse)

Gro-galdr: a conjuration formula to compell a wight to answer

Natt-galdr: night singing, to inhibit night-walking spirits

Lirla-galdr: liltingly sung magic to lull the target to sleep, characterized by rhythm, melody, hummed words, and soft, slurred phrases

Nid: spells to curse or invoke spirits to attack an enemy, often carved on a pole in runes

Runes

Today, runes are best known as a means of divination. But in the lore, it is clear that they were (and are) used in healing and offensive and defensive magic. Our best evidence for the use of runes in divination comes from a passage in *Germania,* which tells how the heads of families decided important questions by casting slips of fruitwood carved with certain signs. We assume those signs were the runes. The oldest known runic inscription was found on a Danish brooch dated around 50 C.E. The runic alphabet, called a *futhark*, from the sounds of the first six staves, most resembles an early alphabet from northern Italy and is probably the result of early contact between Germanic tribes and Mediterranean traders. In the mythology, the runes are the creation/discovery of Odin, who was enabled to "take them up" by a nine-day ordeal hanging on the World Tree. He shared them with the gods, elves and men, though it is not known whether all beings received the same runes.

The most traditional form for the runes used in divination is twigs or slips of wood. Today, most heathens find it more convenient to use wooden discs, ideally pieces they have cut themselves from a branch, or stones. Besides casting the runes on a cloth, they can be laid out in various meaningful patterns inspired by the method used for tarot.

The surviving futharks show many variations, but most modern heathens use the twenty-four-rune "Elder" futhark. The "blank rune" is a modern invention, and most heathens consider its major use to be as a replacement if one of your set is lost. Our understanding of the basic meanings for the runes are derived from the Anglo-Saxon rune poem and the Norwegian and Icelandic rune poems, although the latter cover only the "Younger" futhark. Like the Hebrew alphabet, the runes are not only sounds and signs but also have names and meanings. As a system, the runes are rich and complex. Each one opens the door to an entire area of Germanic culture. Their interpretation is affected by context and situation. Nonetheless, today as in the past, we may attempt to summarize their significance in poetry.

The following is the version I wrote for my book *Taking Up the Runes* (2005):

> ᚠ FEHU is herds and fertile fields,
> Freely, Freyr finds wealth for friends.
> ᚢ URUZ, aurochs, urges earthward
> Spirit strength to shape creation.

ᚦ THURISAZ, the thorn of Thor,
Is force that frees, or fights a foe!

ᚠ ANSUZ, OS, is Odin's wisdom,
Communicating ecstasy.

ᚱ Upon RAIDHO the road is ridden
To work and world around together.

ᚲ KENAZ kens creation's fire;
With torch transforming hearth and hall.

ᚷ GEBO unites the gift and giver
In equal exchange of energy.

ᚹ WUNJO wins Wishfather's blessing,
Joy joins folk in family freedom.

ᚺ HAGALAZ hails ice seeds hither,
Harm is melted into healing.

ᚾ NAUDHIZ is Necessity.
Norn-rune forcing Fate from Need.

ᛁ ISA is the Ice, inertia,
Stasis, and serenity.

ᛃ JERA'S Year Wheel yields good harvest;
Right reward as seasons ripen.

ᛇ EIHWAZ, Yew of Yggdrasil,
Bow of Life and Death, worlds binding.

ᛈ PERTHRO pours its play from Rune cup,
Chance or change for man or child.

ᛉ ELHAZ, Elk is sharp-tined sedge,
Totem power provides protection.

ᛋ SOWILO sets the Sun wheel soaring;
Guiding light by land or sea.

ᛏ TIWAZ is the rune of Tyr;
Victorious victim, enjoining justice.

ᛒ BERKANO, Birch tree, bride and mother,
Brings us earth power for rebirthing.

ᛖ EHWAZ, Eoh, extending energy,
The holy Horse links god and human.

ᛗ In MANNAZ every Man is master;
All Ríg's children are relations.

ᛚ From LAGUZ's Lake life ever flowing
Wells from mother-depths of darkness.

ᛜ INGWAZ wanders the world in his wagon
And dying, leaves life in the land.

ᛞ DAGAZ is a bright Day's dawning,
Life and growth and light for all.

ᛟ OTHALA is holy heart Home
For clan and kin of mind and body.

Runic inscriptions have been found on personal possessions, memorial stones, and labels used by Viking traders. In the sagas, we
have references to their use (especially by Egil Skallagrimsson) in
healing spells, to reveal the presence of poison in a drinking horn,
and to cast a curse. In the *Eddas,* there are references to inscribing
runes on weapons and other items. Unfortunately, although the
uses of runes are described, in most cases the rune to be used is
not stated, leaving plenty of opportunity for research by the
runester. In general, the more you know about the culture and beliefs from which the runes came, the better you will understand
them.

Most modern heathens have some familiarity with the runes and
may use them for decoration as well as for other purposes. Many
begin each day by drawing a rune and meditating on its meaning. A
number of excellent books on runework are listed in the resources
section. For those who wish to pursue more esoteric runic studies,
Edred Thorsson's Rune Gild offers advanced training.

Seidh

The second major division of Northern magic is seidh. These days it is held to cover all kinds of magic involving trance work and skills similar to the shamanic practices of other cultures. Some believe that many of its elements were learned from the Finns or Saami, who have a reputation as being powerful workers of magic in the sagas and folklore. However, such practices are known throughout the Indo-European cultures. The derivation of the word is uncertain—it may possibly be related to *seethe*, as in brewing spells in a cauldron.

Most of the examples given in the Old Norse dictionary refer to the oracular practice described in the *Saga of Erik the Red* and elsewhere. But the term is also used in *Heimskringla* (*Ynglingasaga*, ch. 7), in the list of Odin's powers, where it includes not only prophecy but also the ability to affect the weather, journey in animal form, cause illness and death, and take away or confer power or wit. Seidh might be worked to bring or remove luck and prosperity, promote the fertility of people, animals, and fields (or, in at least one case, to inhibit male virility), and bring luck in hunting and fishing.

Ham-skiptast, or skin changing, is one of the skills included in this area. Except for the berserkers, who took on the persona of bears rather than transforming physically, this seems to have involved a spirit journey in animal form. In *King Olafs Saga* (ch. 37), King Harald of Denmark wishes to find out what is going on in Iceland. His "warlock" journeys to Iceland in the shape of a whale, but is repelled by the local land spirits. In the *Saga of Hrolf Kraki,* the hero Bodhvar Biarki sends out his spirit to do battle in the shape of a great red bear. From Scandinavian folklore we know that everyone was believed to have an animal-shaped fetch that could be perceived by those with second sight. Such lore may also be behind the animal elements in personal names and family totems.

A method used for meditation or possibly spirit journeying in-

volved wrapping up in a cloak and spending several hours in a se-
cluded place such as the space beneath the deck of a ship to work
out a problem. The most famous example of this is the story of
Thorgeir of Lightwater, Lawspeaker (a position somewhere between Speaker of the House and Chief Justice) of the All-thing in
Iceland, who used this method to work out a compromise on conversion to Christianity and save Iceland from civil war. Techniques
that appear to be quite similar are taught today as shamanic or as-
tral journeying.

Familiar from several sources in the lore is the practice of *Uti-seta*,
or Out-Sitting, in which one sits in a sacred place or on a grave
mound (usually at night) to do magic, trance work, communicate
with the dead, and so on. In the "Lay of Svipdag," a young man
who has been cursed by his stepmother sits out on the grave
mound of his mother so that her spirit can counsel him. Magic of
a more active kind was done by singing and dancing on a high
place, such as the roof of a house (in Iceland, buildings had very
thick walls and were roofed with sod, which were sturdy enough
for animals to graze on, so this is not as strange as it sounds). In
Laxdaelasaga (ch. 35), a man called Kotkel and his two sons build
a platform from which to work weather magic against a man they
believe has wronged them, and a storm blows up and their enemy
is drowned.

Other magical practices mentioned in the lore (and in folklore) include spells worked by spinning, twisting, or tying, herb craft, pro-
jecting and removing elf-shot, and providing magical protection.
Anyone with a strong spirit could put the "evil eye" on a person or
animal, sometimes without meaning to. Seidh workers could also
send nightmares, some of which were palpable enough to crush their
recipient. Although battle spells are also worked by galdr, seidh had a
place in warfare, as when the sorceress-princess Skuld works magic
from her seidh platform during the climactic battle in *Hrolf Kraki
Saga*.

Oracular Seidh/Spae

Although the use of runes for divination is not mentioned in the sagas, we have a great many references to the taking of omens and prophecy by other means. Sometimes, this is done by the interpretation of omens. However, the most notable account—in fact the most extensive surviving account of *any* Viking Age religious or magical ceremony—is the episode in which Thorbjorg the "little Völva" prophesies at Herjolfsness in Greenland, given in the *Saga of Erik the Red* (ch. 4). We are told that she sits on a *seidhjallr* (seidh platform), wearing an outfit that includes gear made from catskin, and is put into trance by the singing of a certain song. She then answers the people's questions regarding their current situation and foretells the future life of the girl who sang for her.

Similar episodes appear in a number of other sagas, perhaps because they are a useful literary device for furthering the story. The poems in the *Eddas* in which Odin seeks out the archetypal Völva in the underworld may reflect the way in which the questioning was managed. It is said that the seers, individually or in groups, moved from one district to another rather like a nineteenth-century circuit-riding preacher, and people would gather for the ceremony. In the sagas, we only see the oracular rite being performed by women, but there are references to participation by men in earlier times.

There has been some debate as to whether this form of divination should be classed under seidh, or referred to as *spá* in Old Norse, or *spaecraft*. The scholar H. R. Ellis Davidson calls it seidh in *Gods and Myths of the Viking Age,* and that is the term under which it is most widely known. In my own work, I generally use the term *oracular seidh* to distinguish it from other kinds of seidh magic.

In the early nineties I began exploring ways to reconstruct oracular seidh as a native Northern European magical practice that could serve the pagan community. Since then, my own group, Seidhjallr, has presented the ritual regularly at regional festivals. I have trained individuals and groups who are now practicing in other parts of the United States and the United Kingdom. For further information, see my Web site www.seidh.org. Although not all heathens or heathen groups choose to participate, the practice is now well known and accepted as a part of modern heathen culture.

Deity Possession

One further magical practice should be mentioned, that of taking on the persona of a god or goddess during magic or ritual. I must emphasize that this is *not* a standard part of contemporary heathen practice, and the evidence for it in the lore is uncertain. That said, however it is a human ability, and sometimes, especially if someone is working deeply with a deity and is naturally receptive, it can spontaneously occur.

In *Heidrek's Saga* and *Gautrek's Saga*, Odin appears to have possessed human hosts to accomplish certain deeds. In the story of Gunnar Helming (in *Flateyjarbók)*, a young man is persuaded to pretend to be the god Freyr. He is not, in fact, possessed by the god, but the Swedes he is visiting are apparently accustomed to such practices. When the king sends to bring Gunnar home, it is because "the strongest heathen cults are when living men are worshipped." So god possession may in earlier times have been practiced by priests and priestesses, though it was no longer a regular occurrence during the Viking Age.

Intentional possessory work should only be attempted by those who are already trained in trance work and are working with other trained people. It should never become a substitute for the study of the lore and other ways of working with the gods. Even when a god is speaking, the message comes through the "software" of the human brain and thus may be distorted, and in any case, as heathens, we are responsible for our own deeds no matter who we think we are talking to.

If god possession happens spontaneously, the subject should be grounded by feeding him or her salt or water (or immersing him in it if necessary) and calling back the normal personality by talking about mundane elements in his or her life. If the episode has occurred because the deity has something important to communicate, the connection can be made more safely by spirit journeying (preferably with the support of a friend) to the home of the god.

For more on possessory experience and how to deal with it, see my book *The Essential Guide to Possession, Depossession and Divine Relationships.*

ROUND THREE

Toasts, Boasts, and Oaths

CHAPTER 10

Living Trú

The horn has made its way around the circle for the second time. Janet announces that the third will be an open round, where people can speak as the spirit moves them. About a quarter of the way around the circle, the horn comes to Hárlinda. She is a rather quiet girl who wears a valknut pendant and always dresses in blue or black. Looking very serious, she takes the horn.

"I raise this horn to Odin," she says, holding it high.

"Like that's a surprise," mutters someone and is hushed by his friend.

"To the All-father, wind-rider, breath-giver, master of wit and wisdom, I pray," her voice strengthens. "For years I've been saying I wanted to be a writer, but I always was afraid—afraid I might fail, and even more afraid I might succeed. But I stand before the gods and before you who sit in this hall and say that by this time next year I will finish my novel and send it out, and keep sending it out until it sells or I run out of publishers."

The whisperers have fallen silent. Thorolf nods to Roderic, who gets up and faces Hárlinda.

"We hear you and the gods hear you," he says. "By making this vow in sumble you have bound our fate to yours. If you fail in this, what weregild will you pay?"

"Well, if I can't write the novel, I don't suppose it would make sense to

*offer to write a poem for each of you?" she manages a smile. "Okay. If I
fail in this, I promise I will donate a day of housework to each family in
the kindred."*

*Those who have seen Hárlinda's house raise an eyebrow, but no one
can deny that for her, to spend a day cleaning would be a sacrifice.*

"Your oath is accepted," says Roderic.

"Hail Odin!" Hárlinda drinks from the horn.

A religion serves many purposes for its followers. Through rituals
and spiritual practices, our faith helps us to make contact with the
gods, it creates a community of believers for mutual support and
companionship, and it offers a worldview and guidelines on how to
live. For heathens, the phrase "Live trú" means keeping faith with the
gods, with each other, and with our own true selves. But we do not
act in isolation. We are connected by a web of choices and relationships, and we play our parts in an ongoing cosmic story.

Beginnings and Endings: Cosmology

One of the first questions people ask about a religion is what it
teaches regarding the origin of the world and its ending. Today, the
question of whether the theory of "Intelligent Design" should be
taught alongside that of Evolution is being debated across the United
States. Some have suggested that the problem be solved by teaching
the creation myths of all the world's religions. Such tales do not explain "how" the universe came to be, but they can offer insights into
the "why."

For an account of how the people of the north explained the origins of the world, we turn to the *Eddas*. In the first poem of the *Elder
Edda*, the archetypal Seeress tells us of the beginning of time, "when

nothing was. Sand was not, nor sea, nor cool waves. Earth did not exist, nor heaven on high. The mighty gap was, but no growth" ("Voluspá": 1, quoted in Faulkes 1987, p. 9).

This is elaborated in the "Gylfaginning" (in Snorri Sturlusson's *Younger Edda*), in which a human king called Gylfi visits Asgard and asks many questions. When he wants to know "What was the beginning?" he is told that first there existed what we would think of as two extreme states of matter: Muspelheim, a realm of fire too hot for any human to enter that is guarded by the jotun Surtr, and Niflheim, a place of mists from which flow glaciers—rivers so cold that when they cease to move they become ice, weighted by layer upon layer of rime. Between them lay the great gaping Nothing—Ginnungagap.

When the frozen rime of Niflheim met the fiery sparks of Muspelheim, "... so that it thawed and dripped, there was a quickening from these flowing drops due to the power of the source of the heat, and it became the form of a man, and he was named Ymir." Ymir is the personified Primal Being, human in no sense except that it has a form. As the jotun Vafthruthnir says, he is the "giant in whom all our ancestries converge" ("Vafthruthnismál": 31). Ymir parthenogenetically produced other beings, who became the first elementals, the jotnar of the frost, a concept that might reflect a distant memory of the end of the Ice Age.

However, when the ice melted, another being also emerged, personified as the cow Audhumla, from whose teats flowed four rivers of milk. The cow, who seems to represent a feminine principle, fed Ymir, and as she licked at the icy stones, she released a second being, Buri, who joined with one of Ymir's offspring and became the father of Bor, who was the father of Odin, Vili, and Ve. These figures, evolved from primal forces, were the first true gods. Their names express the concepts of ecstatic awareness, will, and holiness. With them, consciousness appeared, and they began to shape the raw stuff of creation.

The sons of Bor killed Ymir and took his body to the center of Ginnungagap, where they proceeded to recycle all the pieces to make Midgard—the world on which we live. The bones became rock, the flesh became earth, the blood became the seas, and so forth. There are eight other worlds. Niflheim and Muspelheim, of course, were already in existence. We can only speculate about the origins of the others.

But we do know where the other worlds are. Many cultures have maps of what the author Michael Harner calls "nonordinary reality," which may be laid out in the form of a mountain or a tree. In Norse tradition, the cosmos is arranged in the form of a World Tree that is the axis of all the worlds. Though no one knows "from what roots it rises" ("Svipsdagsmál": 14) or when it will fall, it is variously named Yggdrasil or Mimameith and it is the center of everything. Interestingly enough, according to evolutionary biologist Ben Waggoner, rather than being "a march of progress," the process of evolution is more like the growth of a tree, always growing and branching (*Idunna* 58, Winter 2003). Scientists from Charles Darwin on down have used this metaphor, so perhaps there really is a World Tree after all.

Although sources differ on exactly where all the "worlds" are located, their names (or at least the names of the principal places) are well attested. At the top of the tree we find Asgard, the home of the gods. Below it, but still near, is Ljósalfheim ("Light-Elf Home"). Who exactly the Light-Elves are is not entirely clear. They may be the noble dead or spiritual powers that are not quite gods. Next, at the middle of the Tree, we find Midgard, which both is and is not the world we know. The lore tells us that Muspelheim (home of the fire giants) is in the south. Niflheim ("Mist-home"), its opposite, is located in the north. Since Thor speaks of fighting giants in the east, it seems reasonable to put Jotunheim, their home, in that direction. Vanaheim, the home of the Vanir, should therefore be in the west, perhaps over the sea. Going beneath Midgard, we find Svartalfheim ("Dark-

Elf Home"). These may be the dwarves or a shadow version of the bright beings. Deeper still we come to Hel, the destination of those spirits who do not end up somewhere else, and thus the home of most of our ancestors. It should be noted that Hel is not necessarily an uncomfortable place. Odin's son, Baldr, is there, feasting in Hella's hall.

The story of Baldr's return belongs to the end of Midgard's tale. Just as peoples from the Hindus to the Hopi have told of a succession of "Earth Ages," each of which ends with the destruction of life as we know it, in the *Eddas* we hear of the final battle of Ragnarök, the "doomsday of the gods." In that battle, the "Sons of Surtr" (the fire giants) will go to war against the gods of Asgard, bringing with them as allies every other power the gods have fought in the past. Bifrost Bridge will break. The battle ends in a draw, as matched foes destroy, each other but in the process the world itself will be destroyed.

> The sun dims, land sinks 'neath the sea,
> Fall from the heavens the bright stars.
> Steam geysers up, and comes the fire,
> The flames shall leap high to the heavens. ("Völuspá": 57)

Some of the other parts of the prophecy—when the Seeress describes the darkening of the sun and an "axe age, a sword age, before the world falls, a wind age, a wolf age, no man will spare another" ("Völuspá": 45)—sound uncomfortably like a description of world war. But that is not the only way the balance of life could be upset to the point where survivors battle in a dying world.

Mass extinctions of species and changes in earth's climate and ecology have occurred several times in the past. These changes are part of the natural order. On a planetary timescale, our current ecosystem ought to last for many centuries to come. When the time for its ending does arrive, only the destructive forces of nature will remain, and the gods who have become part of human culture will disappear. It is our job to make sure, by preventing nuclear war and environmental degradation, that Ragnarök does not come before its destined time.

Like the mythologies of other cultures, that of the north prophesies a new world that will follow the old. The children of the gods will take over—Baldr will return from Hel to rule—and from beneath the leaves of Yggdrasil two beings, Lif and Lifthrasir, will emerge to repopulate the land. Whether they will be human, as we understand the word, we do not know.

In the cosmology of the north, we have a series of metaphors that resonate with the account offered us by science. We also have the example of gods who, like us, know that their existence will one day end. Unlike us, they know how and by whom they will be brought down. It may be that they will be transformed and reappear in another dimension. But we cannot be sure. What we do know is that we can experience no fear, no uncertainty, that they do not also know. Some have attempted to find in this a millennarian nihilism, but in the joy and courage with which our gods face their ends, we find help when it comes time to face our own.

Wyrd and Ørlög

Everyone is familiar with the image of the three witches, the "weird sisters," cavorting around the cauldron, even if they have never seen William Shakespeare's *MacBeth*. In the play, MacBeth insists on hearing their prophecy, but as is often the case, he does not understand it, and so he brings about his own doom. The question of whether will can overcome *wyrd*, or fate, has been debated ever since the first oracle spoke a prophecy.

In classical myth, the three fates spin, measure, and cut the thread that is the life of a man. Their northern equivalents are the three Norns: Urdh, Verdandi, and Skuld, whose names are all derived from forms of the verb "to be." The first Norn is associated with the "Ur-" or primal nature of a thing, that part of the past that shapes what shall come. Verdandi is the "becoming" part of the equation, the eternally changing present. Skuld is that which *shall be* as a result of what has gone before. At the beginning of Richard Wagner's opera *Götterdämmerung,* we see them spinning the life thread of the world. When it breaks, they know that the doom of the gods has come.

A superficial reading of Germanic lore would suggest that the warriors of old were fatalists, who lay down to die when they saw their doom coming. But a closer reading reveals a much more complex philosophy. To understand wyrd, we have to understand the concept of *ørlög*. Linguistically, this term combines the concepts of "Ur-" designating something primal, a source or origin, and "layer" or "law." In "Völuspá," we are told that the Norns "choose life," meaning that they decide when and where a person will be born, and lay down ørlög, the constraints that will shape that life.

According to Edred Thorsson, the Norns lay down the "primal layers." This concept connects to the image of the Norns dipping up water from the well at the base of Yggdrasil and pouring it to whiten and nourish the World Tree. The Norns may decide the circumstances into which we are born, such as the time and place, and the family with its cultural and genetic inheritance, but they do not determine how our lives will end. As we go through life, more layers are laid down by our own choices, interacting with the choices of all the others with whom we are involved.

We can view ørlög as a series of layers, or as the strands of fate that connect to become the web of wyrd. This is why we must be so careful about the oaths that are taken in the sumble ceremony. The ceremony is sacred space, and what goes on there has an impact in the Otherworld as well as in this one. By bearing witness, we link our own wyrd to that of the oath giver.

There are some things we cannot avoid or change. But we are responsible for the way in which we respond to them. You may inherit a genetic tendency to diabetes, but your choice of diet and lifestyle will determine whether you develop it. You may be born to poverty or wealth, but your own actions will influence whether you end your life rich or poor.

The Afterlife

Germanic religion, like other folk beliefs, was continually evolving and changing. This is nowhere so clear as in its accounts of what happens after death. In the lore, we find a variety of possibilities, depending on time, place, and even individual preference.

The most familiar image of the Norse afterlife is Valhalla, where the warriors chosen by Odin's valkyries fight all day and feast all night. In theory, this fate was reserved for those who died in battle, and of those, only the ones who were particularly brave. At Ragnarök, these are the warriors who will fight at the side of the gods. The lore does hold some indications that Valhalla is more than a home for old fighter-jocks. In the *Saga of the Volsungs* (ch. 12), the dying Sigmund says that he will "go see our kin that have gone before me." That his line is descended from Odin suggests certain families might have a special relationship with specific gods. However, it may not be a matter of choice—it was believed that King Hakon the Good also ended up in Valhalla, even though he was a Christian. In a poem called the "Hakonarmál," we are told how the valkyries Gondul and Skogul brought him to Odin's hall.

But Valhalla is not the only god home to which the dead might go. Snorri Sturlusson tells us that unmarried girls go to Gefjun, and that half the slain go to Freyja. In *Egilssaga*, Egil Skallagrimsson's daughter says she will feast in Freyja's hall. Edred Thorsson suggests that particular friends of the gods may dwell with them in the hereafter—a Thorsman in Thruthheim, a Freyrsman in Alfheim, and so forth.

But not all the dead go to Asgard. Although Snorri lists several "heavens," such as Gimlé, the default setting, so to speak, is Hel, which seems to be the residence of most of the ancestors. I must emphasize, however, that in heathen lore, Hel is not hot, nor is it a place of punishment like the Christian Hell. It is true that Hel includes a region called Nastrond where murderers and oath breakers wade rivers of poison, but Hella's hall, where Baldr dwells, seems to be a cheery place. Today, some heathens believe that Baldr is gathering an honor guard of warriors who will return with him after Ragnarök. We also know that a seeress lives in a mound near the eastern gate. The situation of the rest of the dead is not specified in the lore, but contemporary visionaries see them in camps or villages, where some are willing to speak to those who come seeking wisdom. Certainly, there are episodes in the sagas in which the dead appear to the living in dreams.

Yet, even Hel is not the only option. In the Helgi lays, we hear of a hero who lives in or can return to his grave mound. The practice of burying rich furnishings, food, and so on with the dead implies that some spirits were expected to remain in the vicinity of the grave. In *Eyrbyggjasaga* (chapter 11), Thorolf designates a hill near his farm as "Helgafell" and declares that he will die "into the hill." Some time after his death, a serving man with second sight sees him feasting there with his son, Thorstein, whom they later learn has been drowned. It was also said that some of the kin of Unn the Deep-Minded died into the land. So some spirits apparently choose to stick around and watch over their families, especially if their descendants stay on the family farm. And a word should also be said about those who do not rest easily anywhere. Those who were especially nasty minded in life may cling to the earth and walk as *draugs*, a kind of Norse zombie. Special precautions must be taken to confine them to the grave.

In the Norse view, death is not necessarily a permanent condition. It was believed that many strong spirits choose to return, often to reincarnate in their family line. Several heroes called Helgi were believed to be reincarnations of each other, along with their valkyrie lovers, and King Olaf the Christian was highly incensed when his followers speculated that he might be his ancestor Olaf the Alf of Geirstad come again. This is probably why in Scandinavia it is considered bad luck to name a child after a living relative. Recent scholarship by Winifred Hodge Rose suggests that the soul may have multiple parts, which to to different destinations (*Idunna* 67–69, 2006).

Heathen Virtues

Heathens seek in the *Eddas* and sagas examples and hints as to what a heathen worldview should be and what ethical principles will help us to work with wyrd. Although the establishment of religious laws or commandments is as foreign to heathenism as it is to any other form of pagan belief, in the *Eddas* and sagas heathens can find examples of how to live. In the 1980s, the Odinic Rite in England derived from the old lore a set of guidelines known as the Nine Noble Virtues, which many heathens find useful without feeling bound by them. The Virtues are: Courage, Truth, Honor, Troth ("Fidelity" or "Loyalty"), Self-Rule ("Discipline"), Hospitality, Industriousness, Independence (Self-Reliance), and Steadfastness (Perseverence), to which some add Equality, Friendship, Strength, Generosity, Kinship, and perhaps highest of all, Wisdom. Some also add the six goals of Right, Wisdom, Might, Harvest, Frith ("Peace"), and Love.

The first five Virtues work together to define the heroic soul. We begin with Boldness, or **Courage**, a familiar theme in heroic literature. The word brings visions of Beowulf fighting the monster alone in the depths and returning in triumph, or going up against the dragon as an old man and giving his life to gain the victory. But

Gunther and Hagen are equally heroic when they meet their death at the hands of the Huns. Defeating the enemy, while desirable, is less important than meeting the challenge bravely. The foes we face today are not so obvious, but the resolution required to make hard moral choices is the same. Our ancestors knew that in the end death conquers everyone. What matters is not how long, but how well we live.

To live bravely requires that we value the second Virtue, **Truth**. The greatest heroes see the world clearly. The boasts made at sumble must be based in this clarity, or they may lead to disaster. Sometimes, we must speak boldly, and at other times, truth requires us to keep our own counsel until we are certain, but we must always strive to be as honest as possible with ourselves. For heathens, deciding when and how much to tell family or friends about our religion offers an opportunity to exercise the virtues of both Courage and Truth, although one also needs judgment. To honor Truth also implies that we should be honest in our dealings with others, which is the basis of the next Virtue: **Honor**.

My grandfather was known in his community as an honest man. In another age, he would have been called honorable—he was a man who always tried to do what was right, for whom his word was his bond. We win honor by acting honorably in the expectation that others will act likewise, even when we suspect we will be disappointed. Often, this means following the rules, even when they are inconvenient, though there may be situations in which honor requires one to obey a higher law. Honor is an internal yardstick that holds us to a code of conduct more stringent than any external rules. "Reputation" is what others think of us, but to be honored is not necessarily the same as maintaining inner integrity.

One way in which we prove our Honor is through loyalty, good faith, or **Troth**. Most will have encountered the term only in the old-fashioned wedding ceremony, where it indicates the importance of the vow. Pledging and keeping troth means that you will stay true to your word through thick and thin, that others can both trust and believe in you. It is a word for the sacred bonds between people, and for the bond between us and our gods. An Old Norse word for a patron god was *fulltrúi,* or for a goddess, *fulltrúa,* meaning the fully trusted one. When we keep troth, we not only keep our word to someone we offer help, defense, or whatever else he or she needs.

This is not an easy path. To follow it requires the next Virtue: **Self-Rule**, or **Discipline**. In the sagas, this often involves keeping one's temper when provoked and waiting to take revenge until the time is right. But it has broader implications. The person who can rule his or her own passions can lead others, avoid problems, conserve resources, and make and execute plans. Self-discipline enables us to act courageously and honorably even when we are afraid to do the hard things and sometimes to make the hard choices. As we saw in the discussion of wyrd, our fate is shaped by our choices, and it is discipline that enables us to make good ones.

If the first group of Virtues focuses on individual behavior, the next four Virtues are concerned with our relationship to others. The first of these, **Hospitality**, is one of the most ancient and consistently honored qualities. To offer hospitality was both an obligation and a privilege. In an age and area where there were few inns and no social safety net, survival might depend on the generosity of those who had sufficient resources to offer help. Those who had prospered achieved status by sharing their wealth, which thus circulated throughout the community, the original "trickle down" economy. Today, the network of relationships in the heathen community is strengthened when we welcome those who are traveling. When you are tired from a long drive, it is a fine thing to be met at the door by your hostess with a horn of mead.

To offer hospitality, you must have resources to share, and for that to happen, you must be willing to work hard. For this reason, **Industriousness** comes next on the list of Virtues. Working hard and well is both an old Germanic and American virtue. Benjamin Franklin's advice on getting ahead fits well with the counsel Odin gives in the "Havamál": "Seldom does a lying-down wolf get the lamb, or a sleeping man victory. He who has few workers should rise early, and go himself to work: he who sleeps in the morning will miss much" (58–59). Not all work is for wealth. Volunteer work contributes to the community without necessarily making money. Nor is it required that you become a workaholic. What is important is that the work be done dependably and as well as you know how.

Even though we live in a community of interlocking relationships, we also value **Independence**. Indeed, a certain independence of spirit is necessary if we are to do our share. To be independent does not mean that we don't need others, but it does mean that we are self-reliant. We make our own choices and are capable of action on our own. In practical terms, this virtue means that we should be self-supporting, or, if we are in relationships in which we are contributing in nonmonetary ways, we have the skills to support ourselves and our dependents if there is need. Independence also has a moral and spiritual dimension. Although we learn from elders, teachers, and the lore, we are expected to make up our own minds and reach our own conclusions about matters of faith. Ours is not a religion of gurus.

Last on our list of principal Virtues we find **Steadfastness**. This might even be the most important, since it is the quality most needed if one is to practice the others. To be steadfast is to endure, to persevere, to stick to it, to stay the course, to get the job done. The warriors who watched the Danes coming over the causeway at the battle of Maldon were brave and loyal, but it was steadfastness that kept them fighting beside their lord even when it was clear that hope was gone. This is not a showy virtue, not the kind of thing we think of first when we are talking about heroes, but without it, few heroes would last long enough to win the name. In daily life, this is the quality that keeps us plowing the fields, washing the dishes, paying the bills, and all the other endless, exasperating tasks that win no glory but keep the family or the community going.

CHAPTER 11

Questions and Conflicts

As Karen bears the horn around the circle, the group is treated to a song, a story, a toast from a daughter to her father, and two toasts to gods. Now the horn comes to Barry, and attention sharpens. Barry has the reputation of being a loose cannon, someone who feels that a little conflict keeps people on their toes and is happy to provide it. He has behaved himself so far this evening, but you never know what he is going to do. There was a lot of argument about admitting him to the group, but Thorolf considers him a challenge.

He grins, knowing what they are thinking. "I have a boast to make," he announces, taking the horn.

"You all know that I don't always have a lot of use for the gods. I don't bother them and they don't bother me. I'm not going to apologize. A lot of Viking warriors used to say the same thing. The land wights, and even the jotnar, are another matter. It used to be they could stomp us, but now we're destroying them. The earth is hurting, and we need to pay attention!

"Anyway, my boast is I've been accepted to a graduate program in ecological education at the university, and I'll be starting this spring." He takes a hearty swig from the horn.

"Hail Barry!" Congratulations, mixed with a little relief, echo around the room, and if Thorolf suspects that this is somehow going to end up with the kindred putting in an organic garden, he's been meaning to get around to that anyway.

If pagans in general are an independent-minded lot, heathens are even more so. Anyone who has hung out on a heathen e-list knows that we're fond of, shall we say, "spirited" discussions. Start five heathens talking on any given topic, and you will likely end up with six opinions. The following are some of the areas where the widest range of beliefs may appear.

UPGs and Lore

Ásatrú as a religion is both old and new. Its validity depends on a firm foundation in the lore, meaning information that can be proven or convincingly hypothesized based on historical or scientific methods and criteria using data from literary sources—the *Eddas* and sagas, ancient historians, and to some extent folklore. Secondary sources such as contemporary historians and scholars are useful for understanding the older material. Where available, archaeology can also increase our understanding.

But most people don't find much spiritual nourishment in a bit of rusted iron. If a religion is to live, new ideas are necessary. In heathen circles, the latter are provided by what we call "Unsubstantiated Personal Gnosis" (UPG) a contemporary insight, intuition, or sometimes dream or vision that provides additional and usually unverifiable information about the gods, such as favorite foods or colors. If enough people in different areas come up with the same idea on their own, it may attain the status of modern lore. This might be how the belief that Thor has a red beard became accepted in ancient times.

An example would be the idea that Frigg's colors are white and pale blue. Over the years, people in my group and heathens in other parts of the country have independently visualized the goddess in these colors. Recently, one member was contacted by a man whose primary practice is in the Afro-diasporic tradition who had had a vision of a woman in pale blue and white who said her name was "something like Fricca." Whether the belief of so many has somehow imprinted this idea on the collective unconscious, or Frigg always liked those colors, she certainly seems to like them now.

Different Places, Different Spaces

One source of variation in pagan practice seems to be geography. In Scandinavia, many Ásatrúar see their religious practice as a part of their cultural identity in general, and their connection to their native land in particular. They are reconstructing an ancestral tradition to which they are the heirs. They were brought up on the myths, even though their parents and teachers did not believe in them. Some may even bear the old gods' names. Like Native American tribes who base their claim to certain territories on the fact that their ancestors are buried there, they draw strength from the fact that their forefathers honored the spirits of the land where they lived and died. When an Icelandic writer once interviewed me, the first thing he asked was how we could worship the Norse gods in California.

Like most Americans, I have moved many times and my parents did the same, so this is a problem to which I have given a great deal of thought. Fortunately, though contemporary Icelanders may have ancestral roots in their land, the sagas provide a great deal of information on how those ancestors made their connection with the land when they themselves were newcomers. My answer was that we do the same thing that they did: exploring and sensing the energy patterns in an area, making offerings to the land spirits there, and bringing in our own gods.

The Germans, like the Scandinavians, have an uninterrupted linguistic and cultural connection to their land. However, the Nazi distortions of that heathen past have until recently made it very difficult for them to claim it, and even now they must do so carefully. In recent years, organizations such as the Eldaring have developed a positive heathen practice and begun to gain acceptance by the Scandinavian organizations. During the migrations period Germanic tribes settled everywhere in Europe, so even in those countries that now speak Romance languages, those who become interested in heathenism can claim a tribal connection.

In the United Kingdom, heathens have a variety of options. Descendants of the Anglo-Saxons and the Vikings can claim a Germanic heritage, especially in the south, east, and far north, where archaeological sites and place names bear witness to their presence in the land. However, the British Isles are also exceptionally rich in megalithic remains that predate not only the Germanic but also the Celtic migration into the land. The stone circles and standing stones provide a focus for connection to the land spirits that is accessible to pagans of all traditions.

Although in ancient times a religious practice that focused on local and ancestral spirits may have been more common, in the sagas we do find individuals who are known for their devotion to specific gods or goddesses. This kind of relationship is often found among English heathens today and is even more prevalent in the United States and Canada.

Even within the U.S., differences occur. In general, heathens on the East and West Coasts, especially New York and San Francisco, are the most liberal. New Englanders have the reputation of being independent and egalitarian, while Texans seem to favor more hierarchy. The midwestern heartland is more conservative, with a higher proportion of families in kindreds. Heathens in the West, whether liberal or conservative, are very individualistic.

Earth Religion

It is clear from the sagas that in the old days people honored and worked with a variety of beings, in some cases even more closely than they worked with the gods. These included the wights of the land on which they lived. As in most traditional cultures, the polytheistic beliefs of the peoples of the north shaded into animism, an awareness that all things have spirits. They lived in a world in which there was a wight in each crag and waterfall, in every grove and field.

Just as the Japanese term *kami* includes the spirits of places and things, in the north anything that has an identity may also have a resident wight, from a ship to a barn. The brownie of English folklore or for that matter the house elves of the Harry Potter books are cousins of the Norwegian *nisse* and the Swedish *tomte,* to whom offerings of porridge are still made on Christmas Eve. Of course, not all wights are friendly. The trolls are to be feared, except, perhaps, when they are co-opted. In Seattle, a cement troll sits beneath one end of the Fremont Bridge, and when the San Francisco Bay Bridge was rebuilt after the Loma Prieta earthquake, construction workers made an iron troll and placed it inside one of the supports to keep the bridge from falling down again.

The question of which beings were honored besides the gods brings us to the question of whether heathenism should be considered an earth religion. As defined in the Wikipedia, a grassroots online encyclopedia, *earth religion* is a New Age term used mostly by believers in neopaganism and similar faiths. It is an umbrella phrase that is used to cover any religion that honors the earth, Nature, or fertility gods, such as the various forms of Goddess worship. Some find a connection between Earth worship and the Gaia theory (en.wikipedia.org/wiki/Earth_religion). In interfaith work, it may be used as a term that includes both native or tribal religions and neo- or reconstructed pagan traditions. My own definition of an earth religion is one whose adherents recognize that they depend on the web of life of this planet for survival and act accordingly.

To someone growing up in a traditional culture, whether in ancient Europe or contemporary Africa, the term would be meaningless. In such environments, the power of Nature and the survival value of living in harmony with natural forces is too obvious to need a name. It must be admitted that the success of such a lifestyle varies, depending on the resources of the environment and the knowledge of the culture. Ancient cultures, from Greece to Iceland, were just as capable of damaging their ecosystems as modern ones are—it is just that today we can do it much more quickly and completely. By contrast, environmental science gives us the tools to understand what has happened, why it happened, and sometimes what we can do about it.

In the larger pagan community, the term "earth religion" often seems to be accepted without examination. Many pagans work hard to maintain an ecologically responsible lifestyle. Most try to at least recycle, but some seem to feel that honoring the earth in seasonal rituals excuses them from having to make sacrifices to preserve it. In reconstructing traditional practices, heathens must not only figure out what they meant to our ancestors but also which of them we can and should bring in the modern world. For those of us who no longer live in intimate daily contact with Nature, it is easy to ignore the fact that everything we use came from somewhere, even if it only reaches us after going through several levels of processing. But because it now takes a conscious effort to honor the spirit in all things, we have the opportunity to do it mindfully.

What does heathen lore have to teach us about our relationship to the earth? Like other pagans, many heathens believe in an animate universe—the idea that everything, from stones to stars, has spirit. To this day, the Icelanders will route roads to avoid moving rocks known to be inhabited by alfar. All the Germanic peoples reverenced sacred trees and pools.

Although most North American heathens focus their religious practice on the gods and goddesses, the spiritual ecology of the northern world included a broad spectrum of spiritual beings, and although, as we have seen earlier, some of them, such as the nisse, tomte, or brownie, were concerned with human activities, a majority were spirits of the natural world who are the great elemental powers. The great forces of Nature, the jotnar (giants), rule the wild places and the elements, such as the mountains and glaciers, wind and sea. In the myths, they are the first generation of beings from whom spring the gods, and from whom the gods seek brides. Dangerous and powerful, they are shape-changers and wisdom-givers.

Whether they are good or evil depends on the context. To those directly in its path, the hurricane is a disaster, but farther inland its storms may bring much-needed rain. Today, we are most likely to see the jotnar in disasters in which the forces of Nature are out of balance. Fishermen on the Indian Ocean sensed a malign energy in the oncoming tsunami. Those of us who saw the firestorm in the Oakland Hills could feel the voracious greed of the Sons of Surtr as the flames marched down the hills. Some believe that the mythic battle of Ragnarök will take place at the end of the Age when the current ecosystem has become so unbalanced that only the destructive jotnar remain. We can only hope that human activity will not shift that balance before its destined time.

In the *Eddas* and sagas, we have stories in which the gods interact with humans, and stories in which they interact with the giants, but no tales in which the giants interact directly with humans unless, like Skadhi, they have been brought into the world of the gods by marriage. The gods mediate between us and the giants, but humans can work directly with the *vaettir,* the wights who are attached to field and grove, hill and waterfall, to ensure luck in hunting or fishing and the fertility of the land. As elsewhere in Europe, in Iceland belief in these beings persisted even after the conversion to Christianity. They became the lesser elves and fairy folk and were honored with offerings, as they still are today.

The gods themselves were concerned with the earth's fertility. Although the Vanir—Freyr and Freyja, their father Njordh and their (probable) mother, Nerthus, are the deities most obviously associated with the productivity of ocean, pasture, and field, Thor, the son of Odin by the earth-giantess Jordh, brings the rain, or holds off the storms, and on the Continent, Wodan was invoked at harvest time. While Njordh seems to have been a god of getting wealth from the sea, Nerthus, known to us from much older Roman-period sources, was a goddess who blessed the fields. We have in addition some Old English prayers and charms that address Earth as a divinity.

The prayer of an early English herbalist begins: "Holy goddess earth, parent of all things in nature, who all things generates, and regenerates the planet which thou alone showest to the people" (Harley 1585, 24; in A. Storms [1974], p. 312). Other Old English charms invoke Earth equally with sky. However one interprets the "Erce, eorthan modor" of the Aecer-blôt spell, the invocation that follows is certainly addressed to the earth, and when the first furrow is driven, the farmer says:

> *Hal wes ôu, folde, fira modor,*
> Hail to thee, earth, mother of men
> *beo du growende on Godes fæôme,*
> Be thou fruitful in God's protection,

fodre gefylled firum to nytte.
with food filled, men to benefit.
     (Cotton Caligula A VII,ff.17; 6a–178a; in
     A. Storms [1974], p. 177)

Even at a time when it was forbidden to call on Thor or Odin, the church could not prevent the farmer from invoking Mother Earth for bread.

One of the few formal prayers surviving from the Viking period is found in the "Lay of Sigdrifa" in the *Elder Edda* (one of the sources on which Wagner drew for his *Ring* operas). After being awakened by Sigfrid, the Valkyrie greets the world by saluting the day and the night, goddesses and gods, and "holy earth who gives to all" ("Sigdrifumál": 2). This reverence for holy earth, she who "gives to all," surely qualifies heathenism as an earth religion.

Ethnicity and Culture

Besides differing in organizational structure and cultural focus, contemporary heathen groups may also vary from restrictive to inclusive in their attitude toward the relationship between religious faith and ethnic identity. Those who believe that becoming heathen is a return to the faith of our ancestors, and that only those who have Germanic ancestors ought to be interested, are labeled "Folkish," whereas those who feel that the religion should be open to all who are called by the Germanic gods are called "Universalist," or more properly, "Inclusive." Heathenry is not the only branch of paganism to be challenged by an inherent conflict—Wicca has to deal with the potential tension between a belief in gender equality and a theology based on sexual polarity. For heathens, the question is how to reconstruct a religion based in northern European culture without racism.

In any religion derived from a single culture, the question of the relationship between culture, ethnicity, and faith may arise. Unlike missionary religions such as Christianity, Islam, and some sects of Buddhism, pagan traditions do not go out looking for converts, nor do they believe that their faith ought to be practiced by everyone. Originally, like Judaism, the pagan traditions belonged to specific tribes and cultures, and one joined by being raised in or adopted into the religion. Christianity became a worldwide religion because pagans left their native religions or were forcibly converted. Logically, people born into a missionary religion should have the right to convert back again.

But to which pagan tradition should they return? Some seek the religion of their ancestors. This is the choice made by many Native Americans who are trying to reclaim their culture. In Greece, Hellenic reconstructionists are doing the same and are opposed by the Greek Orthodox Church, whose leaders know that the gods of Olympos are still embedded in the Greek psyche and fear their power. In Scandinavia, the Aesir are part of the cultural heritage and are reclaimed along with native folkways. In Denmark, heathenism is called *Forn Sed* (Olden Ways).

In Scandinavia, where immigrants represent a relatively small percentage of the population, few who are not ethnically European are likely to seek membership in an Ásatrú kindred, nor is anyone going to accuse those whose fathers and grandfathers fought the Nazis of trying to become a superrace. In Germany, where rediscovery of the native cultural heritage nourished the emerging nationalism that was distorted into such an evil growth by National Socialism, the question is of prime importance. In North America, whose population continues to swell with successive waves of immigrants, many of whom are non-European, it presents an ongoing challenge as well.

But the Olympian deities are also worshipped by many in Europe and North America, and the Aesir and Vanir seem quite happy to migrate to places never mentioned in the old lore. Just as the West Norse carried their gods with them to Iceland, we have brought them to the New World. Many contemporary heathens are drawn to the religion because they have ancestors from England, Scandinavia, or Germany. Those of us who have envied the Native American tribal identity find it very rewarding to explore our Native European roots. However, between the fourth and eleventh centuries Germanic peoples wandered from Greenland to North Africa. Later, their descendants spread throughout the Americas. If Germanic heredity is needed to make a connection with the heathen gods, these days almost anyone, regardless of physical appearance, might possess the required genes.

In the heathen community, there has been a great deal of discussion of the relationship between genetics and religion. My observation is that language and culture have a far greater influence on people's religious affinities than does genealogy. Genetic studies in Europe seem to indicate that the Indo-Europeans did not arrive in sufficient numbers to make much difference in the physical makeup of the population. What changed was the culture.

If the host culture is strong, as in Roman Gaul, it can absorb invaders like the Franks and later the Normans both culturally and linguistically. In the United States, a succession of immigrating ethnic groups have been absorbed into the American melting pot, progressing from ghetto to neighborhood to assimilation. Some families have made the effort to preserve elements of their native culture while others have not—the degree to which a culture is retained often depends on whether there are enough members in a given area to form a community—but within three generations, their children are able to blend into the American mainstream.

The English language and democratic political structure have proved to be successful in the global village, which has made elements of all contemporary cultures available all over the world. Some of the current tensions in the Middle East are caused by local fears that the global culture will replace their own. This availability can be seen as a threat or an opportunity. To choose a new path requires one to take responsibility for one's actions in a way that staying safely within one's birth culture does not.

I attribute the current accessibility of the Germanic gods in the English-speaking world to cultural inheritance. They live in our names for the days of the week, and in the basic structures of our institutions and culture. A majority of those who have been drawn to Germanic religion are of European descent. Of course, that is also true of other pagan religious traditions, such as Wicca. I suspect that the reason owes more to culture than ethnicity—the growing popularity of "alternative" or "new" religious movements seems to represent a disenchantment with the dominant WASP culture. Thus, Asian or African Americans may also find themselves drawn to pagan religions. Just as non-Indians who wholeheartedly adopt Native American culture may be accepted by some tribes, members of other races who are called by the gods of the north may be welcomed into some heathen kindreds, while others refuse them.

I believe that a culture of diversity offers many choices, including the option to select the best from an older culture and reinterpret it in ways that will work in a new environment. This is what heathens who follow the reconstructionist pagan paths are doing today. I have come to believe that in matters of religion, the configuration of our bodies is far less important than that of our minds and souls. When I meet someone who reads the same books, does the same rites, and honors the gods as I do, it is the meeting of minds that identifies her to me as spiritual kin. Many paths lead to the Northern Way, and the gods know their own.

Ásatrú and Wicca

When someone starts looking for an alternative to monotheism, Wicca is often the first pagan tradition they encounter. Since Wicca is the best-known form of European polytheism, and certainly has received the most publicity (not always accurate), it seems wise to offer a quick comparison of the two. Bear in mind, however, that there are many varieties of both Wicca and heathenism, so not everything said here will universally apply.

The major difference between Wicca and Ásatrú is that where Wiccan rites may invoke deities from several cultures, heathens stick to gods and goddesses from the Germanic lands. In addition, where Wicca is usually duotheistic and archetypal, seeing all female deities as aspects of the Great Goddess, divided into the archetypes of the Maiden, Mother, and Crone, and all male deities as aspects of the Horned God (if the male principle is even acknowledged), Heathenry is more straightforwardly polytheistic, worshipping a range of gods and goddesses who all come from the same culture, are equal in status if not in popularity, and can stand alone without need for a male or female complement.

In Wicca, the spirits of nature are organized according to the four elements of earth, air, fire, and water. Heathen cosmology features fire and ice as opposing principles. The giants and lesser wights are grouped according to location and function—frost giant, barn wight, and so on—rather than element. Occasionally, the four dwarves who uphold Midgard in the four directions might be called as part of a hallowing, but elemental invocations are not a standard part of the procedure.

Although as more people become interested in paganism, in general and in Wicca in particular, the latter is developing a laity, traditional Wiccan covens are intimate, closed groups whose purpose is to develop their members spiritually and magically through a series of initiations. Everyone eventually becomes a priestess or priest. By contrast, most heathen kindreds are modeled on a family or household. Some members may specialize in Germanic folk magic, as others become experts in brewing, woodcarving, or other skills the group needs, but the purpose of the group is to provide spiritual community. The kindred may offer rites of passage, but these tend to mark life changes rather than magical achievements. Only one or two members study to become clergy, if the kindred has any official clergy at all.

There also tend to be considerable differences in ritual style. Wiccan practice is partly descended from medieval ceremonial magic, and its rites are often also magical workings. For this reason, most ceremonies include a rather elaborate preparation and warding for the circle, which can, in extreme cases, take more time than the working it wards. Even in those Wiccan traditions that are eclectic and improvisational, the basic structure is usually there. Heathen rites are modeled on folk practice, which is generally much less formal. The major exception would be for certain heathen magical rites such as rune workings and seidh (see chapter 12).

Wicca, especially those varieties descended from the Gardnerian tradition, observes a strict cycle of ceremonies consisting of regular "esbats" held at the full moon and seasonal "sabbats" marking the solstices, equinoxes, and cross-quarter days. The latter are usually celebrated as mystery plays illustrating the myth of the season. Although such plays, based on the lore, are sometimes featured in heathen rituals, and the great feasts mark the turning of the seasons, the connection is a loose one.

Where heathenism tends to be much more formal and precise than Wicca is in its relationship to the lore. This is partly because in the Germanic tradition we *have* a great body of lore with which to work, whereas Wicca is essentially a modern tradition (albeit a very successful one—see Ronald Hutton's *Triumph of the Moon* for a history of its evolution). Ásatrú has often been referred to as "the religion with homework," and adherents are encouraged to read the primary sources as well as scholarly works discussing them and debate their meaning rather than accepting interpretation by others. Although personal insights and intuitions are considered useful, they are not received as authoritative. If a modern myth or interpretation of the lore does not fit the historical facts (where those can be demonstrated), it will not be accepted regardless of how useful it may be. Many heathens study Old Norse or Anglo-Saxon so that they may examine the sources in their original languages.

Another difference between heathenism and Wicca is in the way in which ethical principles are articulated. Where Wicca has a single Rede, "An it harm none, do what ye will," and the law of threefold return (whatever you do will come back to you tripled), heathens mostly hold to the Nine Noble Virtues (see chapter 10). Where Wicca has a simple statement of what not to do, heathenism offers a more elaborate statement of what one *should* do.

Although both traditions draw people from a broad range of beliefs and cultures, Wiccans as a group tend to be more politically liberal, even countercultural, and more tolerant socially and sexually than heathens, except in Iceland, where Ásatrú is associated with the political Left. Although there are plenty of heathen liberals, and at various points the heathen spectrum merges into the Goth, biker, and ceremonial magic communities, the average heathen group is more aligned with middle America, with a strong emphasis on family values, and many heathens are conservative both politically and socially. In fact, contemporary heathenism displays much the same spread of opinions one finds in the United States today. So far, a shared devotion to the religion has enabled liberals and conservatives to work together—one hopes that this success can be taken as a good omen for the survival of the country and world to which we belong.

Almost all Wiccan ceremonies include a circle casting, calling the quarters, and invocation of a goddess (and god). Heathen groups may hallow the hall in some way, but not everyone even goes that far. Because Wiccans have considerable leeway regarding which gods and goddesses they call on, it is possible for a coven to retain a Wiccan ritual style while focusing on the Norse gods, though the goddesses rather resist being forced into the traditional boxes of Maiden, Mother, and Crone. Some heathens denigrate such practices as "Wiccatru." I doubt that the gods themselves care about the style in which they are worshipped, though I believe that they can be more completely understood and perceived more clearly when honored in a Germanic cultural context.

CHAPTER 12

From Hearth to Hof:
Heathen Organizations

Karen has almost reached the end of the circle. She gives the horn to a wiry, middle-aged guy with grizzled hair pulled back in a ponytail. He goes by the name Sven the Axe and handles the horn like an old friend.

"In the first round we hailed a lot of folks from our history," he begins. *"I've been through a lot of it myself. I remember when nobody could have imagined a party like this, much less throw one. I've been a follower of the old gods since the sixties, and seen our history being made. I've met a lot of the Big Names in Heathenry—Thorsson, McNallen, and the rest. But you know, it's not the people who write about the religion but the people who live it that make the difference—all the heathen folks like you who make our religion live."* *He pauses and coughs, clearly a little surprised himself by what he's said.*

"My toast is to Raven Hammer Kindred, and to Thorolf and Janet, who have housed us and fed us and listened to us patiently for so long!"

"Hail Thorolf!" People rise to their feet with the cry. "Hail Janet!"

"Raven hammers forever!" The tables reverberate as pewter tankards and knife hilts thunder approval.

From Lone Wolves to Den Mothers

When I first encountered Ásatrú in the 1960s, the typical follower of the Norse gods was a young single man whose ideas about the religion had been formed, at least in part, by reading *Conan* and *The Lord of the Rings*. He was attracted by the heroic ideal and usually had a sword hanging on his wall. Admittedly, the fact that most of the young men I knew were in the Society for Creative Anachronism may have had something to do with this perception, but Stephen McNallen, the founder of the Ásatrú Folk Assembly, has said that books and movies led to his discovery of the Norse gods as well. This stereotype of a heathen as a gung-ho warrior type is common in the larger pagan community to this day.

Eventually, however, the young men began to find partners and settle down, and Heathenry became a community of families. During the past forty years, an increasing number of women have become interested in Ásatrú. Prudence Priest reports that in the early days, when she and her friend Pasha showed up at a gathering, everyone cheered because there were "so many women." Today, although heathens may have a more positive attitude toward masculine energy and the warrior spirit than some other pagan traditions, heathen kindreds are strongly supportive of families and family values, and women are taking leadership roles. In the Troth, the organization I know best, two of the six presidents have been female, and men and women are represented equally on the board.

The other major change has been the shift from solo to group practice, or from families to kindreds. This term, which was popularized in the 1970s by the Ásatrú Free Assembly, has become the most commonly used term for the heathen equivalent of a coven. In the old days, most heathen religious practice was centered in the home. This is still true today. Many of the holidays are celebrated with and for the immediate family. However, just as in the old days the household included those who worked on the land, distant relatives who needed a home, and sometimes a stranger or two from another country who needed a place to stay for the winter, the family members who gather around the fire today may be a "kindred of intention," bound not by blood but by belief.

Some groups, harking back to the household as the ancient focus for religious practice, may call themselves *hearths*. In the Troth, a group led by a trained godman or godwoman (Troth clergy) is a *garth*, referring to the safe space guarded by the walls of a Viking farmstead. A building devoted to Ásatrú worship may be called a temple or a *hof*. Like other pagans, most heathen groups meet in people's living rooms; however, in the United States several hofs have been built on private land.

It is probably still true to say that the majority of kindreds are independent, but an increasing number of groups and individuals are finding benefit in association with a larger organization. To join some of these organizations, like the Ásatrú Alliance, one must be a member of a member kindred. Others accept individual members only. Still others, like the Troth, define membership individually, but maintain a list of kindreds run by members. The Troth also has regional stewards who provide information and help in networking.

Even Christianity, with its ideal of one holy church with a single ritual and creed, has evolved many interpretations of its doctrine and variation in religious practice. Pagan religions exhibit even more variety. Just as in the old days each region—sometimes even each family—practiced its own version of the ancestral religion, one can find a great deal of diversity in focus and practice among heathen groups today. What they all share is a belief in the Germanic goddesses and gods.

Organizational Styles

Many heathen kindreds consist of a nuclear family and a friend or two, with no formal organization at all. Where the leaders are energetic and meeting space is available, a group may grow to thirty or more. A very few groups have been able to designate a separate building as a hof (the equivalent of a dedicated church edifice). An average kindred size seems to be around twelve to fifteen. In general, the larger the group, the more structure is required. Some remain informal and open, while others have a strict hierarchy with formal procedures for becoming a member. Groups vary also in exclusivity. In some, other affiliations are irrelevant so long as they are left at the door, while some kindreds require that a member belong to their group alone.

An Ásatrú kindred may include anything from a single family to a community of several dozen, led by a gothi (priest) and/or gythja (priestess). It may be limited to the members of a single family or draw from an entire region. Leadership can be elective or rotate among the membership, and some kindreds have no formal leader, but most often the gothi or gythja is the person with the energy and inspiration to found the group and keep it going. Often a gothi will start a kindred first and later seek formal clergy training from an organization such as the Troth.

Most groups are autonomous in regard to internal structure and practice, although rituals may be shared among groups in the emerging traditions. In regions with a dense population of heathens, kindreds may divide into groups that remain allied, or kindreds in an area may cooperate to put on festivals. However, even those groups that choose to join a national organization such as the Ásatrú Alliance, or to be listed by the Troth, retain their independence.

Many kindreds offer a ritual that is the equivalent of a Wiccan initiation, though not all require it. In some kindreds, members must renounce the practice of other traditions, while in others, multiple affiliation is accepted. Most groups are familiar with and honor the Nine Noble Virtues (see chapter 10), but not all work with a formal statement of belief.

Ásatrú kindreds gather, usually on weekends, to celebrate seasonal festivals or to hold blóts (a ritual with a specific purpose) or sumbles (a ritual honoring gods, heroes, and ancestors), as described in chapter 8. Most kindreds observe the Winter Nights (a feast at the beginning of winter that honors the ancestors), Yule, spring, and midsummer feasts mentioned in the sagas. Other blóts and days of remembrance are listed on the religious calendars developed by organizations such as the Odinic Rite and the Ásatrú Folk Assembly, but are not universally observed. Many kindreds also sponsor regular classes and study groups in Norse mythology, crafts, the runes, and other aspects of the culture.

Traditions

As suggested earlier, European heathens tend to base their practice on the cultural traditions of their own lands. In North America, however, options are more open. Because the bulk of the surviving information comes from the Old Norse *Eddas* and sagas, most Ásatrú kindreds base their practice primarily on this lore, call the gods by their Old Norse names, use Old Norse terminology in ritual, and focus on the versions of their myths set down in Scandinavia. One of the early leaders to take this approach was Stephen McNallen (see the discussion on the AFA later in this chapter), whose rituals were among the first to be published and had a great influence on those who followed. Theodism, a style based on Anglo-Saxon practice was created by Garman Lord.

Theodish heathenism tends to be more formal, both in organization and philosophy, than Ásatrú. Members are linked by a network of mutual oaths and may work their way upward through several ranks of hierarchy as they learn and take on more responsibility. Leaders of newer groups may be in a feudal relationship to the leaders of older ones.

Finding a Kindred

When people first discover Ásatrú, they are often convinced that they are the only heathens in town. There are a number of ways to change this situation. The easiest is to join a national organization, especially if it has regional representatives or sections. You will find a list of such groups later in this chapter. Heathens also meet each other through e-lists sponsored by organizations or special interest groups. National or regional pagan festivals and conferences such as Starwood in New York and Pantheacon in California include heathen events in their programs. If you cannot find an existing kindred in your area, you may still encounter other seekers like yourself who would like to form one.

At least at first, you may have to be willing to travel considerable distances to interact with other heathens. Some people only do so at the annual moot or festival. However, you can also make a try at recruiting people. One way to begin is by starting a "Norse Mythology Study Group." Post announcements at local colleges and bookstores. If there is a pagan community, post it on its hotline. By the time you have worked your way through the tales of the gods, you should be able to tell who would be interested in encountering them in a more personal way.

It may take you awhile to find a group that is a good fit. It is always wise to avoid making a commitment until you are sure that you are not only compatible in personality but in values. Not having any people of color as members in a group does not prove that they would not be welcome if they applied, likewise for people of different gender orientations, but too much emphasis on traditional gender roles and concern about the number of immigrants coming into the country might be a warning sign. As I have stated before, although many heathens are attracted to Northern Paganism because of their ancestry, the gods call whom they will.

Heathen Clergy

One question that has stimulated a great deal of lively discussion in the heathen community is whether we need trained clergy. Heathen tradition certainly supports the concept of "a priesthood of all believers." In a family based religious structure, the father and mother act as priest and priestess to their household, leading worship and making the offerings. However, the lore offers other possibilities.

Medieval Iceland divided the country into political districts, each of which was represented by a *gothi*, a word that also means priest. In practice, the gothi was both: he represented his neighborhood both to the All-thing and to the gods. The gothi was the most respected person in his district, whose leadership qualities and luck drew other men to swear allegiance to him. He was also the one with the resources to host the great seasonal feasts at which men made offerings to the gods.

Although today's heathen clergy have no civil responsibilities, they are still the people whose energy, creativity, and commitment to the gods drive them to found kindreds and inspire others to follow them. However, once they have taken on the responsibilities of leadership, they often find that others are expecting them to act, not like a tenth-century gothi, but like a twenty-first-century minister. The culture in which we all grew up has a certain image of what a religious leader is and does, and we bring our preconceptions with us when we convert to the new religion.

So a modern gothi or gythja (feminine) may be asked not only to plan group rituals and teach the lore but also to conduct weddings and memorial services and offer pastoral counseling. To interact with representatives of other faiths on an equal basis, they need to know something about theology. For this reason, people who have become heathen religious leaders may feel a need for further training. At present, the only training program for heathen clergy that I know of is sponsored by the Troth.

One area in which heathen leaders may become involved is interfaith work. For some, this means interacting with other kinds of pagans by attending festivals, participating in Pagan Pride Day festivities, and the like. Some have an opportunity to get involved in interfaith activities with people from other religions. To do this effectively, they need to keep an open mind, be articulate about the history and beliefs of Ásatrú, and know enough about the beliefs of other faiths so that they can state ours in a way others will understand. They must also be prepared to explain why a "heathen religious tradition" is not a contradiction in terms.

Another specialty is prison work. According to some estimates, there are more heathens inside prison than outside it—I should emphasize, however, that most of them did not become Ásatrú until after they got there. In recent years, incarcerated heathens, like Wiccans and Native Americans, have been making progress in gaining recognition and the right to worship together, and a number of prison kindreds exist today.

Inmates turn to heathenism for a number of reasons. The emphasis on courage, endurance, and personal responsibility can be a great inspiration to those who are living in an extremely hostile environment. It is also true that in an institution, survival may depend on making alliances along ethnic lines. I have been told by one former inmate that some prison authorities encourage racial tensions as a way of dividing and controlling the inmate population. Nonetheless, although prison kindreds are unlikely to be integrated, many exist on terms of respect, if not warm friendship, with other ethnic groups and faiths.

Because many prisons are located in remote areas, finding heathen clergy who can work with these groups is difficult. Many heathen

leaders are already overworked trying to keep their own kindreds going and simply do not have the time, or they live too
far away. Often, all that can be done is to provide books and other
educational materials. Understandably, some heathens on the outside have reservations about getting involved. However a number of
heathen clergy have begun prison programs, and we are beginning
to learn how it should be done.

Heathens Online

The spread of information on Germanic religion has been aided
to a great degree by the Internet. If you type in "Ásatrú" as a
search term, Google will give you 2,540,000 hits. This of course is
not limited to actual Web sites sponsored by groups or
organizations, but it does suggest how much information is out
there. Many heathen individuals and groups are unaligned, but
increasingly, they are banding together into larger associations,
some representing distinct heathen "denominations," and others
serving as alliances of diverse groups linked by philosophy rather
than by style of practice. When even well-established religions
have their sects, denominations, and heresies, it is not surprising
that modern Heathenry includes a diversity of practice and
opinion.

Surviving Your First Heathen Event

By the time you've finished this book, you may have made
contact with a heathen group or be hoping to do so. Sooner or later,

you will be invited to participate in a sumble. Experienced heathens will probably laugh at this list, but if you are new, it may help you to avoid some problems that would affect your enjoyment. Every suggestion made here is based on someone's hard experience. I would like to thank the participants in the Troth members' e-list who read the first version and contributed additional suggestions.

If you are new to Heathenry or new to the kindred you are visiting, ask your host or hostess what the etiquette for this event will be. A guest who brings an offering for the feast or a gift for his or her host, or who offers to help clean before or after the event, and who tries to understand and adapt to the "culture" of the host kindred, will always be welcomed.

- When you are offered the horn in sumble, turn it so that the tip is pointing down or somewhat to the side before drinking. If for some reason you cannot or should not drink alcohol, you may kiss the horn to honor it, pour a little on your finger and dab it on your forehead, or (if you are outside) pour a little on the ground. Ask your hosts which they would prefer. If the horn is being carried around the circle by a "valkyrie", hand it back to her. If not, hand it to the person next to you.

- You can make your prayer silently or softly, and then say "Hail!" Never say anything derogatory or insulting in sumble, especially about one of the gods or goddesses.

- Remember that while in sumble you are symbolically sitting at the Well of Wyrd. What is said in sumble affects not only your fate but also that of everyone present, so be very careful what you say and how you say it, especially in a statement of intent that could be taken as an oath.

- Just as you should not invoke deities from other pantheons in a heathen sumble, avoid turns of phrase from other traditions, such as "A Elbereth Gilthoniel," "Blessed be," "Merry meet," "Amen," or "Hallelujah." (The only exception might be at an interfaith event, or if you are attending sumble as a representative of another tradition. In either case, discuss what you plan with your host or hostess.)

- In some groups, the custom is to stand when making a toast. In others, you may sit, or you may choose. Ask your host what the group's preference is.

- Ask if you should keep your own cup or horn filled and whether you should drink only when someone makes a toast.

- Know your capacity. In an open-ended sumble, the horn may go around many times, and the alcohol content of mead can be a lot higher than it seems. If you have had enough, when your turn comes honor the horn instead of drinking.

- If you wish to honor the wights, refer to them as land or house wights, land spirits, landvaettir, and so on when speaking aloud so that no one thinks you are toasting the "white people."

- Do not talk while someone else is making a toast. If you have to leave the sumble, do so while the horn is being transferred from one person to another.

- In a round for the gods, stick with deities from the Germanic pantheon. If you are not sure if a deity is appropriate, ask your host. You should also ask your host whether it is permissible to honor Loki, or even to mention him. If you are uncertain about honoring a particular god or goddess, you can say "Hail the Aesir and Vanir!" or "Hail the Elder Kin!"

- In a round for the ancestors, the person you honor should be dead. If heroes are also included, you may toast a living person, but do state whether the person is alive or has passed. Do not honor a character who is known to be fictional, no matter how much you admire him or her. Beowulf is all right, but probably not Xena (although you could toast the actress who plays her). A default toast is "Hail the ancestors!" or "Hail to the Alfar and Dísir!"

- In some kindreds, the third round is for stories or songs. If so, keep it brief and to the point. A generic toast for the third round might be "Hail the host!" "Hail the folk!" or "Hail to those who sit in this hall!"

- Ask before touching or using anyone else's horn, ritual gear, or weapons.

- Hospitality is a heathen virtue, but so is being a good guest. Take care of your stuff, offer to help clean up, and don't drink all the beer. If you have dietary issues, check on the menu ahead of time or bring something that you know you can eat.

Organizations

Heathenry in the twenty-first century is alive and well, with an online presence for organizations old and new. Googling "Heathen Organizations" will get you current URLs for the most active groups both here in the U.S. and in Europe. They vary widely in political and social philosophy. For a list of groups that have taken a public stand against racism, see the list of Inclusive Heathen Organizations posted by Heathens Against Hate, www.heathensagainst.org/inclusive-heathen-organizations. Personally, I would recommend the Troth (www.thetroth.org), an inclusive international Heathen organization with which I have been associated for many years. Membership gets you the journal, *Idunna*, and access to a members' e-list where people from all over are happy to discuss ideas and experiences and answer your questions.

Resources

A First Book List

BASIC TEXTS

Faulkes, Anthony, trans. *Edda*. London: Everyman, 1987. Also known as the *Prose Edda,* this is the most complete translation of the first retelling of the myths and lore.

Hollander, Lee, trans. *The Poetic Edda*. Austin: University of Texas, 1986. The most widely available translation of the mythological poems. The language is somewhat flowery, but it works well in ritual.

Orchard, Anthony, trans. *The Elder Edda: A Book of Viking Lore*. London: Penguin Classics, 2011. More recent accurate but less poetic translation.

The Sagas of the Icelanders. London: Penguin, 1997. A dozen of the most important sagas and six tales. Written within a century or so of the events they chronicle, the sagas are our best source of information on how people of the Viking Age lived and thought. They are also fun to read.

PRACTICE OF HEATHENISM

A Book of Blóts. Berkeley, CA: The Troth, 2004 (P. O. Box 1369, Oldsmar, FL 34677) A collection of articles about heathen ritual construction and examples of rituals for every occasion.

Chisholm, James. *True Hearth*. Smithville, TX: Rûna-Raven Press, 1993, www.geocities.com/runegildusa/RunaRaven. Rituals and practices for the heathen household.

Gundarsson, Kveldulf, ed. *Our Troth,* Vols. 1–2. A new multivolume 3rd
    edition is in preparation.
————. *The Teutonic Way* (contains *Teutonic Religion, Teutonic Magic,*
    and *The Road to Valhalla*). New York: Saga Press, 2018.
Krasskova, Galina. *Exploring the Northern Tradition.* Franklin Lakes, NJ:
    New Page, 2005. An accessible introduction to the gods and ways to
    worship and work with them, also a good source for information on
    Theodism.
LaFaylive, Patricia M. *A Practical Heathern's Guide to Ásatrú.* St. Paul, MN:
    Llewellyn, 2013.

NORTHERN MAGIC
Aswynn, Freya. *Northern Mysteries and Magic.* St. Paul, MN: Llewellyn,
    1990. An introduction to rune work from a mystical perspective.
Kodratoff, Yves. *Nordic Magic Healing.* Forlag, Norway: Universal Publish-
    ers, n.d., www.nordic-life.org/nmh. Healing practices using bind
    runes and energy techniques.
Paxson, Diana L. *Taking Up the Runes.* Boston: Weiser, 2005. An introduc-
    tion to the runes with meditations, rituals, and spells for each one,
    along with a survey of related myths and culture.
————. *The Way of the Oracle.* Boston: Weiser, 2012.
————. *The Essential Guide to Possession, Depossession, and Divine Rela-
    tionships.* Boston: Weiser, 2015.
————. *Odin.* Boston: Weiser, 2018.
Thorsson, Edred. *Futhark.* Boston: Weiser, 1988; *Runelore.* Boston: Weiser,
    1987; and *At the Well of Wyrd.* Boston: Weiser, 1989. These three
    works introduce the theory and practice of runelore. For more works
    by Thorsson, see the Rûna-Raven Press, www.geocities.com/runegildusa/
    RunaRaven.

CULTURE AND STORIES
Crossley-Holland, Kevin. *The Norse Myths.* New York: Random House,
    1981. A good introduction to the Norse myths and legends.
Davidson, Hilda R. Ellis. *Gods and Myths of the Viking Age.* New York:
    Barnes & Noble, 1996 (originally issued by Penguin as *Gods and*

Myths of Northern Europe, often available at used bookstores in college towns). Also look for *The Lost Beliefs of Northern Europe*. New York: Routledge, 1993, or anything else by this author.

Lindow, Jon. *Norse Mythology*. New York: Oxford University Press, 2012.

Heathen Music

CLASSICAL

One of the best ways to get in tune with a culture is through its music. Wagner's Ring operas are not only inspiring, they qualify as primary sources for the evolution of our mythology. From Scandinavia, we have the works of Edvard Grieg and Jan Sibelius. Since the appearance of the first Rosensfolle album in the early 90s Nordic folk music has become wildly popular, and Viking Metal also has an enthusiastic following. To explore, search for any of the groups listed below on YouTube (this list is just a beginning). Start with any of these and YouTube will suggest more.

Wagner, Richard. *The Ring of the Nibelungs* (*Das Rheingold, Die Walküre, Siegfried, Götterdammerung*). Especially the Metropolitan Opera production, available on DVD with subtitles from Deutsch Gramophon.

Wagner's *Ring* operas remain the most notable example of heathen religious music. Singers have been known to describe that performing in the operas was "a religious experience," and heathens who like classical music are devoted fans (although we have had to forbid the singing of the "Call to the Mists" from *Das Rheingold* at moots, as it tends to summon rain). The work of Edvard Grieg, Johen Halvorsen, Jean Sibelius, and other composers of the Scandinavian "nationalist" schools can also be used at kindred meetings to set the right mood.

FOLK, FOLK ROCK, AND "VIKING METAL"

Look for albums by Nordic Roots, Krauka, Väsen, Gamarna, Skald, Nordisk Sang, the German group Corvus Corax. Traditional groups with a more mystical flavor include Heilung, RavenSkul, and Wardruna (they did the music for the Vikings TV series). For metal, try Black Hat Society (hauk.bandcamp.com), Led Zeppelin, Amon Amarth.

GROUPS TO LOOK FOR

Leaves' Eyes, Frigg and Germany's Falkenbach (who pioneered "Folk Metal"). Viking Metal is represented by Bathory, Enslaved, and Einherjer. Folk Metal by Aly Bain and Ale Moller, the Finnish group Amorphis, and the Norwegian Bukkene Bruse. For a more ancient sound, there are groups such as Krauka and the Sequentia ensemble, led by musicologist Benjamin Bagby, which specializes in presentations of ancient material such as the *Eddas* and *Beowulf* with medieval instruments.

Information, Publications, and Gear

BOOKS

Anglo-Saxon Books, www.asbooks.co.uk
Northvegr Foundation, www.northvegr.org
The Troth, www.thetroth.org, also publishes the quarterly journal *Idunna*.

STATUES

Sacred Source, www.sacredsource.com

MUSIC

General information, groups.yahoo.com/group/havamal_ studies
Nordic Roots Music, www.noside.com

PODCASTS

Saga Thing, sagathingpodcast.wordpress.com
Dr. Jackson Crawford. Jackson Crawford's Old Norse Channel
     www.youtube.com/watch?v=XqaRcmEgJNw
Gifts of the Wyrd, giftsofthewyrd.podbean.com

Bibliography

Anthony, David W. *The Horse, the Wheel and Language.* Princeton University Press, 2007.

Bauschatz, Paul C. *The Well and the Tree: World and Time in Early Germanic Culture.* Amherst: University of Massachusetts Press, 1982.

Blain, Jenny. *Wights and Ancestors.* Devizes, UK: Wyrd's Well, 2000.

Bonewits, Isaac. *Witchcraft: A Consise Guide.* Earth Religions Press, 2001.

A Book of Blóts. Berkeley, CA: The Troth, 2004.

Calico, Jefferson F. *Being Viking: Heathenism in Contemporary America.* Sheffield, UK: Equinox, 2018.

Cleasby, Richard, and Gudbrand Vigfusson. *An Icelandic-English Dictionary.* Oxford, UK: Clarendon Press, 1874.

Dumézil, Georges. *Gods of the Ancient Northmen.* Berkeley: University of California Press, 1973.

Faulkes, Anthony, trans. *Edda.* London: Everyman, 1987.

Geary, Patrick J. *Before France and Germany: The Creation and Transformation of the Merovingian World.* New York: Oxford University Press, 1988.

Gelling, Peter, and Hilda R. Ellis Davidson. *The Chariot of the Sun and Other Rites and Symbols of the Northern Bronze Age.* New York: Praeger, 1969.

Gundarsson, Kveldulf, ed. *Our Troth.* Vol I and II. Charleston, SC: Booksurge, 2006.

Greer, John Michael. *A World Full of Gods: An Inquiry into Polytheism.* Tucson, AZ: ADF, 2005.

Griffiths, Bill. *Aspects of Anglo-Saxon Magic.* Norfolk, UK: Anglo-Saxon Books, 2003.

Grimm, Jacob. *Teutonic Mythology.* New York: Dover, 1844.

Hollander, Lee, trans. *The Poetic Edda.* Austin: University of Texas Press, 1986.

Hutton, Ronald. *Triumph of the Moon: A History of Modern Pagan Witchcraft.* New York: Oxford University Press, 2004.

Idunna 63 (Spring 2005).

Kvideland, Reimund, and Henning K. Sehmsdorf, eds. *Scandinavian Folk Belief and Legend.* Minneapolis: University of Minnesota Press, 1988.

Lynch, Laure, *Othroerir,* LuluPress, 2005

Manco, Jean. *Ancestral Journeys: The Peopling of Europe from the First Venturers to the Vikings.* London: Thames & Hudson, 2013.

McNeill, Florence Marian. *The Silver Bough III.* Glasgow: William Maclellan, 1961.

Morris, William, trans. *Volsungasaga.* New York: Collier Books, 1962.

Musset, Lucien. *The Germanic Invasions: The Making of Europe.* New York: Barnes & Noble, 1993.

North, Richard, ed. *The* Haustlöng *of Þjóðólfr of Hvinir.* Middlesex, UK: Hisarlik, 1997.

Pálson, Herman, and Paul Edwards, trans. *Eyrbyggjasaga.* New York: Penguin, 1972.

Paxson, Diana L. *Brisingamen.* New York: Berkley Books, 1983.

———. "Earth Religion and the Troth of the North." *Mountain Thunder* 6 (1992), www.hrafnar.org/norse/hail-earth.html.

———. "Freyja." *Sagewoman* (Summer 2002).

———. "Frigga." *Sagewoman* (Fall 1994).

———. "Sex, Status, and Seidh: Homosexuality in Germanic Religion." *Idunna* 31 (1997), www.seidh.org/articles/sex-status-seidh.html.

———. "Sif." *Sagewoman* (Summer 2005).

———. "Worshipping the Gods." *Idunna* 20 (1993). www.hrafnar.org/norse/worship.html.

Price, Neil S. *The Viking Way: Religion and War in Late Viking Age Scandinavia.* Uppsala, Sweden: Uppsala University, Department of Archaeology and Ancient History, 2002.

The Sagas of Icelanders. London: Penguin, 1997.

Sawyer, P. H. *Kings and Vikings: Scandinavia and Europe, A.D. 700–1100.* London: Methuen, 1982.

Schnurbein, Stefanie von. *Norse Revival: Transformations of Germanic Neopaganism.* Leiden: Brill, 2016.

Snook, Jennifer. *American Heathens: The Politics of Identity in a Pagan Religious Movement.* Philadelphia: Temple University Press, 2015.

Spanuth, Jürgen. *Atlantis of the North*. London: Sidgwick and Jackson, 1979.

Speer, Albert. *Inside the Third Reich: Memoirs*. New York: Macmillan, 1970.

Steigmann-Gall, Richard, *The Holy Reich: Nazi Conceptions of Christianity, 1919–1945*. Cambridge, MA: Cambridge University Press, 2003.

Stenton, Frank M. *Anglo-Saxon England*, 3rd. ed. Oxford, UK: Clarendon Press, 1971.

Sturlusson, Snorri. *Heimskringla*. New York: Dover, 1990.

Sykes, Brian. *The Seven Daughters of Eve*. New York: Bantam, 2001.

Tacitus. *The Complete Works of Tacitus*. Ed. and trans. Moses Hadas. New York: Modern Library, 1942.

Thorsson, Edred. *Futhark: A Handbook of Rune Magic*. New Beach, ME: Weiser, 1984.

Wagner, Richard. *The Ring of the Nibelung*. Trans. Stewart Robb. New York: Dutton, 1960.

Wallace-Hadrill, J. M. *The Barbarian West, 400–1000*. Oxford, UK: Blackwell, 1985.

Index

Great Migrations, 17–26
  conversions to Christianity,
   36–44
Greek Orthodox Church, 154
Greenland, 32
Greenland Saga, 32
Greer, John Michael, xii
Gregory, Pope, 37
Grendel, 24
Grimm, Jacob, xv, 15, 46
Grimm's law, 18
Gro-galdr, 119
Gudrod's Day, 113
Gudrun, Kriemhild, 25–26
Gulltopp, 57
Gundarsson, Kveldulf, 52, 90–91,
  114, 174–75
Gunnhild, 40
Gunnlodh, 62–63
Gunther, 141
Gylfi, 61
Gythja, 167–69

Hagen, 141
Hakon, Jarl, 33, 112
  Day, 112
Hakon I (the Good), 40–41, 138
Hallinskidhi, 57
Halsing. *See* Invocations
Hammer Rite, 105
Ham-skiptast, 123–24
Harald Bluetooth, 40, 123
Harald Hairfair, 40
Harner, Michael, 134
Harvest, and Sif, 88
Haunebu, 15–16
"Haustlöng," 77–78

Hearths, 163
Heathen, use of term, xi, xii
Heathen faith, overview of, x–xii
Heidrek's Saga, 126
Heimdall, 56–58, 74
Heimskringla (Sturlusson), 13, 30,
  47, 123
Hel, 135, 139
Hella, 72, 75, 93–95
Hellenic traditions, xii
Helmet plates, 28
Helming, Gunnar, 126
Helvetians, 19–20
Hengest, 22
Henry VIII, 44
Hera, 81
Hermann (Arminius), 20, 44
Hermann (Arminius) Day,
  113
Hildisvini, 90
Himinbjorg, 56–57
Himmler, Heinrich, 49
Hitler, Adolf, 49
Hlín, 84
Hofs, 163, 164
Hollander, Lee, 102
Holmgang, 59
Holy days, 109–13
Home altars, 103–4
Homer, 14
Homosexuality, and Freyr, 68
Honor, as heathen virtue, 141
Hopt, 118
Hörn, 90
Horned God, 157
Hospitality, as heathen virtue,
  142